THE AUTHORITY
GIVEN TO MANKIND

THE AUTHORITY
GIVEN TO MANKIND

By Mark R. Anderson
www.markandersonministries.com

Published by:
Mark Anderson Ministries
P.O. Box 66
Cody, WY 82414-0066 USA
Email: goodnews@vcn.com
Phone: 307-587-0408

ISBN-13: 978-1985034723
ISBN-10: 1985034727

Book design/layout by Gabriel Arosemena, GEA-designs

Special acknowledgements and thanks to:
- Sharmila Anderson my lovely wife and helpmate for transposing and editing, adding many thoughts or expounding more thoroughly to this book.
- Faith Kingston, our main contributing editor.
- Contributing editor- Dr. Paul Bergamini.
- Unless otherwise indicated, all scripture quotations have been taken from the New King James version of the Holy Bible. The Holy Bible, The New King James version Copyright © 1979, 1982 by Thomas Nelson, inc. other translations used are as follows: (NIV) New International version, (Amp) Amplified, (ASV) American Standard version.
- Scripture quotations taken from the Holy Bible, New International Version. Copyright © 1973, 1978, 1984 by International Bible Society. Used by permission.
- Scripture taken from the Amplified Bible. Copyright © 1962, 1964 by Zondervan publishing. Used by permission.
- Scripture quotations taken from the Holy Bible, American Standard version.

ENDORSEMENTS

This book embraces a life that is surrendered to Jesus, coupled with powerful grace. Mark takes a simple, theological vantage point as he discusses the authority God has happily given to people so they might co-labor with Him. The Authority Given to Mankind ties the theology with numerous scripture references and testimonies that demonstrate the truths that are discussed. The testimonies are beautiful and powerful and fun to read! You will be blessed to see the practical demonstration of authority and emboldened to see it reproduced in your life.

— Steve Backlund , Bethel Church Redding, CA
www.ignitinghope.com

I have known Mark for more than 30 years. In fact, I met him for the first time at a gym when I heard him crying for help as the weight he was benching was pressing down on his chest threatening to crush him. Mark is an adventurous man who is always tackling things bigger than he is. He has learned over the years the authority God gives us and has depended on the Holy Spirit to put it into practice. He has taught on this subject all over the world for the last 30 years. You will love this book which is drawn from scripture, and his own many personal experiences. It will help you to overcome!

— Pastor J.R. Polhemus, The Rock Church Castle Rock, CO

The gospel brought from heaven by Jesus Christ is the greatest thing the earth has ever seen! It brings restoration to what's been broken, healing to what's been damaged, strength to what's been weakened, and eternal life to those entrenched in darkness. Somehow, over the centuries, the church at large has lost the working knowledge of the power and authority that still lives strong in Jesus' gospel. Mark Anderson's new book will bring this back into focus for you! The Lord will work with you and your church, too, "confirming the Word with signs following." Mark 16:20

— Steve C. Shank, Founding Pastor of City on the Hill Ministries and Confirming the Word Church Based Bible Schools

My husband, Dr. George Hill, and I recommend this book to each and every person who wants to receive a miracle. It is a book that will increase your faith for the supernatural. Mark Anderson is a modern day evangelist and has been a tool in God's hands to heal many. The testimonies in this book are from real people who trusted a supernatural God and received their miracle! Yes, Jesus is still in the miracle business!

— Dr. Hazel Lurline Deborah Hill, VCI Missions Director
www.victoryint.org

The Authority Given to Mankind has the power to transform your life and those around you. Mark has written a divine manual with a clarion call to help you inhabit your birthright. All who give ear and heart to the revelation in this book will have the opportunity to experience the reality of His kingdom in their every day life.

— Dennis Reanier , Author of Shaking Heaven and Earth
www.revivalcry.com

For the last 20 years I have watched the Lord use Mark greatly in healing ministry. Mark lives what he has written in this book every day. I would recommend this book to any believer who wants to grow in their understanding of spiritual authority.

— Pastor Ron Kingston, Cody Christian Church, Cody, WY
Founding Member of Cowboys With A Mission, Meeteetse, WY
(Ron is Mark's Pastor in Cody and former professional bull rider)

Mark Anderson lives what he teaches. In his latest book, *The Authority Given to Mankind,* Mark creates faith in the reader with powerful testimonies, plus lays out a biblical foundation for understanding what God offers to His people. This one needs to be read by all!

— Dr. Harold R. Eberle, President Worldcast Ministries

The Authority Given to Mankind

TABLE OF CONTENTS

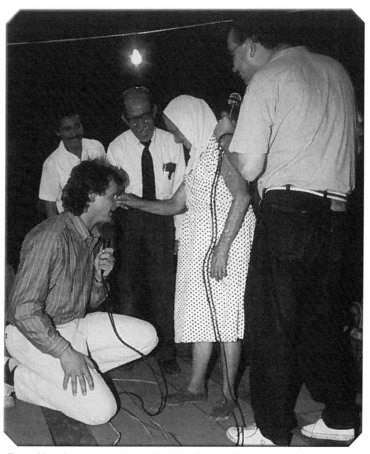

Rosa Altamirano - completely blind for 22 years. Demonstrates healing after Jesus opened her eyes - **Chinandega, Nicaragua 1994.**

CHAPTER 1

Mankind's God-Given Authority

We have taught on the subject of our God-given authority to ministers and church leaders throughout the world. As they acted upon this teaching, we have received reports of many miracles and salvations as villages and cities see Jesus alive. Once we comprehend our God-given authority and partner with Holy Spirit to ensure its application in the physical realm, we too can experience miracles, signs and wonders on a regular basis. I will share first about the dominion and authority given to mankind versus passively accepting everything good or bad in life as God's will. We have the choice or free will to believe the Word of God and Jesus' theology, which is the best theology any believer could embrace (see John 1:1 & 14, 6:38, 14:9), or we can just passively accept all religious traditions passed down as truth, without seeing if it lines up with what Jesus taught or what the Word says.

First I will share how this teaching has impacted leaders. From 1991- 1993 I was one of the main speakers at the Sowers Ministry annual ministers conference held in Kathmandu, Nepal, at the largest church in Nepal at that time. Leaders from India, Nepal, Bhutan and other countries attended the conference. I taught on the subject of authority. During this time only 1/5 of 1% of Nepal's population was considered Christian. Nepal was strictly a Hindu kingdom at this time. Many undeniable miracles occurred from the first day of the conference and continued each day. During the first teaching the Holy Spirit drew my attention to a minister in the middle of the audience and I asked him to come up. He had been totally deaf for 6 years and was from India. I said "this is how authority works. I will command a deaf sprit to come out and Holy Spirit will open his ears." I placed my hands on his ears and said "In the name of Jesus I command you deaf spirit come out in Jesus' name. Ears open and hear in Jesus' name." Immediately his ears opened. I told the 150 ministers there they could operate in the same way.

I shared with these leaders that they could exercise authority over sickness and demons. They put this into practice at the conference and saw immediate results. In the evening we opened the conference up to the public. Anywhere from 250 to 600 people showed up each night. Two people who were close to death were instantly healed as well as many others as we all prayed with authority in Jesus' name.

The leaders continued to pray and use their God-given authority after the conference. Many of them prayed for people as they journeyed back to their homes and saw many healed. They also prayed in their villages and towns, seeing a tremendous outpouring of Holy Spirit as they put God's Word into practice. After two of these ministers returned to their village Jesus appeared in the sky over their village and the entire village saw Him. The villagers wondered who this was and the leaders who returned from the conference shared that it was Jesus. The entire village came to Christ! Before the conference many of the leaders had never seen a miracle or healing. After the conference miracles and healings became a regular occurrence all over Nepal as Christ was preached with authority.

When I traveled back to Nepal six years later to speak at a conference, I found that the statistics had changed. Now 3% of Nepal's population were considered Christian. I asked how this change had come about. I was told it is because of all the miracles that Jesus is doing in Nepal. Miracles have become a regular occurrence there. John 6:2 says, *Then a great multitude followed Him* (Jesus), *because they saw His signs which He performed on those who were diseased.* Jesus' miracles drew many people to Himself. It is no different today. Hebrews 13:8 says, *Jesus Christ is the same yesterday, today and forever.*

In April of 2001 my son Reed, I and others trekked up to the village of **Deusa, Nepal** (Mount Everest Region) to conduct a 4-day healing outreach and leadership conference in a village church pastored by Krishna Bahadur. Pastor Krishna had attended the conferences in Kathmandu in the early 1990's and in 1999. He trekked many days on foot and travelled by bus to make it to the conference each time he attended. He had spent time in prison and had been beaten severely for his faith in Jesus Christ before we met him. Seeing his commitment, I told him someday we would come to his village and minister.

We stayed in the village 'Allstar Hotel' (another name for a hotel where you can see all the stars at night through the holes in the roof). Many deaf and mute people were healed in this outreach, including twin brothers who were born deaf and mute. They both could hear immediately and one brother could repeat words we spoke. One minister had trekked for two days on a broken foot to attend our outreach and training. One of our team members, Mike Okulski, prayed over him and he was instantly healed and overwhelmed by the presence of God, and tears began to stream down his face. One day Maoist soldiers passed through and we hid upstairs in the hotel until they left.

Holy Spirit has moved powerfully in that region and now there are over 200 house churches in the Mount Everest region of Nepal. Pastor Krishna has been a big part of that movement. Latest statistics in Nepal reveal it is now around 10% Christian and has the fastest growing Christian population in the world per capita. Nepal is no longer a Hindu kingdom. Despite persecution, freedom of religion is now allowed.

The Authority Given To Men And Women In The Beginning

Lets look at the dominion and authority given to mankind in Genesis 1:26-28 says, *And God said, "let us make **man in our image,** after **our likeness:** and let them have **dominion** over the fish of the sea, and over the fowl of the air, and over the cattle, and over all the earth **and over every creeping thing that creeps** upon the earth. So God created He Him; male and female He created them. And God blessed them, and God said unto them, be fruitful, and multiply, and replenish the earth, and **subdue it:** and have **dominion over** the fish of the sea, over the fowl of the air, and over every living thing that moves upon the earth."*

The word **likeness** in the Hebrew means an **exact duplication in kind.** *Therefore become imitators of God [**copy Him and follow His example**], as well-beloved children [imitate their father]* (Ephesians 5:1 AMP). Jesus spoke this world into existence and put within us the same power and authority to speak things into existence. ***Death and life*** *are in the* ***power of the tongue,*** *And those who love it and indulge it will eat its fruit and* ***bear the consequences of their words*** (Proverbs 18:21 AMP). In order to walk in His likeness and in our God-given authority we need to understand the power of our words. We have seen many thousands healed through the name of Jesus in our outreaches overseas. Most of those people are healed without laying hands on them, just speaking life into their bodies, cursing sickness, infirmities and disease and commanding their bodies to line up with God's word. James 3:6 (Amp) tells us that our tongue *sets on fire the course of our life [the cycle of man's existence].* So much of what we are experiencing in life, good or bad, was brought on by what has come out of our mouth. With our tongue we exercise our God-given authority to bring life or death into the earth. We are made in His likeness, to imitate Him, to do what He does, and to see the same results.

Psalm 115:16 says, *The heavens, even the heavens are the Lord's: but the* ***earth hath He given to the children of men.*** In the beginning God gave man the authority and dominion to rule over everything on this earth. God said I will take control of the entire universe but I will put you, mankind in charge of this little speck in the universe called earth. Genesis 1:26-28 states that man was made in God's image to have dominion.

I love what Psalms 8:3-6 (Amp) says. *When I see and consider Your heavens, the* **work of Your fingers,** *The moon and the stars, which You have established, What is man that You are mindful of him, And the* **son of [earthborn] man** *that You care for him? Yet You have made him a* **little lower than God,** *And You have crowned him with glory and honor.* **You made him to have dominion over the works of Your hands;** *You have put all things under his feet.* The first thing to see in these verses is that this earth was given to the **'children of men, son of man or the earthborn'** I am a child of a man or son of a man. So are you. The ones born on earth, the earthborn are the ones who have dominion and authority. Dominion literally means **to rule, to be the ruler and reign over the earth, over every living thing.**

Hebrews 2:8 Amplified expounds more on Psalms 8:6 *You have put all things in subjection under his feet [* **confirming his supremacy**]. *"Now in putting* **all things in subjection to man, He left nothing outside his control.** *But at present we do not yet see all things subjected to him.* Here it states man was given supremacy and nothing was left outside of his control. This shows very clearly that man has dominion and authority on this earth. Mankind should not sit back passively and let things happen on this earth, doing nothing with the dominion and authority he or she has been given. The **choices mankind makes with his or her freewill** will either have impact for good or evil. God is not to be blamed for the evil in this earth, but mankind has a responsibility before God to govern this earth with prudence. We will be judged by what we do with the dominion and authority given to us by God in this lifetime. Do we use it for good, remain neutral, passive or do we use it for evil? There is a responsibility that comes with this dominion and authority given by God. Jesus said *From everyone to whom much has been given, much will be required; and to whom they entrusted much, of him they will ask all the more* (Luke 12:48 Amp). What are you doing with the authority you were given by God? Are you helping make this world a better place?

God gave authority on Earth to those who were born here or are the children of men. In order to have authority on the earth Jesus had to strip Himself of His deity and come to earth to operate in the authority of man, born on earth. Notice how many times Jesus referred to Himself as the Son of Man versus referring to Himself as the Son of God, even though He was the Son of God. This is so important to understand if you want to know how to operate in the authority given to mankind.

How did Satan come in the beginning of time? He came in the form of a serpent (see Genesis 3:1) **"creeping upon the earth."** In Genesis 1:26 God had given Adam and Eve authority *over every creeping thing that creeps upon the earth.* Adam succumbed to Satan's lies and gave his authority over to

Satan. Satan then became the "**god** or the ruler **of this world**." (See 2 Corinthians 4: 3-4). Mankind and the earth were cursed because of sin (disobedience). Poverty, sickness, demon infestation, death and all forms of evil began to take place after Adam's fall (see Genesis 3:16-19).

I want to show you something Satan said to Jesus when he was tempting Him in the wilderness. *Then the devil, taking Him up on a high mountain, showed Him all the kingdoms of the world in a moment of time. And the devil said to Him, "**All this authority** I will give You, and their glory; **for this has been delivered to me,** and I give it to whomever I wish. Therefore, if You will worship before me, all will be Yours"* (Luke 4:5-7). Where did Satan get this authority? Adam and Eve gave it to him when they submitted to his lies. That is how he became the god or ruler of this world and still is to this present day (see 2 Corinthians 4:3-4). Mankind forfeited his position to Satan. Jesus never yielded to Satan's temptation but took back our authority by going to the cross, dying, defeating Satan in hell, and rising from the dead. Thank God for the second Adam who got back our authority and gave it back to us when He was raised from the dead. *And Jesus came and spoke to them, saying, "**All authority has been given to Me in heaven and on earth*** (Matthew 28:18). Psalms 115:16 says *the heavens are the Lord's: but the **earth hath He given to the children of men.*** Jesus Christ, God the Creator also became a

19

man born on earth in order to have authority in heaven and on earth. If Jesus has all authority how much authority is left for Satan, demons, sickness, and infirmities? None! Jesus took back the authority we gave to Satan and passed it back to us (see Matthew 28:19-20 & Mark 16:17-18).

One other thing God told us to do in Genesis 1:28 was to **subdue it:** *and have* **dominion over.** The word **subdue** means to conquer, master, control, keep in check, restrain and bring into subjection. Without understanding what Jesus, God the Creator did for mankind in Genesis 1:26-28 we will never rise up and walk in the authority that he gave us (anyone born on this earth).

Young boy was given up to die. Instantly healed by Jesus in our first outreach to **Nepal - Kathmandu 1992.**

Getting ready to trek with my son Reed and others to **Deusa, Nepal, near Mount Everest** region to do 4 day outreach - **April 2001.**

Historic **Leadership Conference Kathmandu, Nepal Spring 1992.** Once conference was over many miracles, signs and wonders broke out all over Nepal as leaders returned home.

Twins born deaf mutes healed. Able to hear for the first time in their life. One began speaking - **Deusa, Nepal, near Mount Everest.**

This Pastor from India attended the first leaders conference I conducted in **Kathmandu, Nepal in 1992** for the Sowers Ministry. He was completely deaf for 7 years. After taking authority over a deaf spirit in Jesus' name his ears were instantly opened. He returned next year to testify he could still hear clearly.

Benjamin - Attended our conference and outreach in Kathmandu, Nepal for the purpose of mocking us. What he saw that night radically changed his life. He witnessed the undeniable miracles of Jesus and gave his life to Christ. He went from being a trouble maker in school to being the smartest student in the entire High School. He later went to Christ for the Nations Bible School and became the leader of the Sowers Ministry in Kathmandu.

21

Mary Spethman - had a titanium 2"x3" plate and screws in her knee for 35 years. She was finding it hard to walk. She received prayer, her knee was on fire and was healed by Jesus. Doctor could not find the titanium plate. It had disappeared! - **Casper, Wyoming, USA.**

CHAPTER 2

Extreme Sovereignty Ditch And Greek Philosophy

When the righteous are in authority and become great, the people rejoice; But when the wicked man rules, the people groan and sigh (Proverbs 29:2 AMP).

When the righteous rise up in authority and humility to rule whether in government or to use their authority for healing, miracles or deliverance people will rejoice and praise, glory and honor will go to our great God. But if we do not understand authority and it's importance in society the wicked will fill that void and the people will groan and complain. Let me share with you one the biggest stumbling blocks in western Christianity in rising up with the authority that was given to mankind.

Many Christians who are heavily into the "sovereignty of God" message say that if you have a free will and exercise your authority to command sickness and demons to go it is the same as telling God what to do. Where is mankind's place on this earth? We will look at **SOVEREIGNTY** in depth. What is sovereignty? Most Christians will say God is Sovereign! This is correct but what does that mean? I will quote from Steve C. Shank's excellent book *Schizophrenic God? Finding Reality in Conflict, Confusion, and Contradiction* published by Destiny Image (best book I ever read on this subject matter). *"Most people believe that God is sovereign; and of course, if God is God, He is sovereign. Webster's American Family Dictionary (New York: Random House, Inc., 1998) defines sovereign as "having supreme rank, power, or authority." In other words, He's at the top of the ladder. There is no one above Him. God is also **omnipotent**, which means He's all-powerful, possessing unlimited power. He's also **omnipresent**, which simply means He's always present everywhere."* But does that mean that God has omni-control over the earth and mankind has no say in the matter? Let's look at this and see what is truth, as found in the scriptures and where does the balance lie with the subject of the sovereignty of God.

Some Christians take the sovereignty of God too far and feel that they are supposed to just sit back and let God do everything. They also think that whatever happens in life, good or bad, is God's will, because God is sovereign. This reduces Christianity to the same level as Islam or Hinduism, which believe that whatever happens in this life good or bad is Allah's will or the will of the Hindu gods and your karma in life. Karma is the Hindu's version of sowing and reaping, there is no grace involved. Why do so many Christians believe the same and have such a misunderstanding of the sovereignty of God? **Sovereignty simply means having supreme rank, power or authority.** I do believe in the sovereignty of God. Once again what does it mean God is sovereign? He is the ultimate ruler, the head, the top one, the one with the most power and authority! That is the place of God the Father, God the Son Jesus Christ and God the Holy Spirit. But to whom did they give the earth, to rule, reign, subdue, and have dominion over? To mankind! Psalm 115:16 says, *The heavens, even the heavens are the Lord's: but the **earth hath He given to the children of men.***

A lot of the 'extreme sovereignty' views came about when Augustine, who was a Greek scholar, came to Christ and interjected Greek philosophy into Christianity. This is what most Christians in the West believe today, knowingly or unknowingly. They embrace Augustine and John Calvin's doctrine (Calvinism) more than what Jesus or the early church taught. Augustine, Calvin and Luther brought much good into Western Christianity, but at the same time had a very distorted view of the nature of our Heavenly Father because of the influence of Greek philosophy. All of these great men of

God had tremendous hunger to know God more and tried to pass that on to others. Augustine put great emphasis on being more spiritual because his desire was to be closer to God. Martin Luther brought about the revelation that the just should live by faith and not by works. That revelation had tremendous impact on the Body of Christ for the better.

One good thing we have learned from Greek philosophy is to study, ask questions and reason. The Greeks believed in testing things and proving something if they were so. 1 Thessalonians 5:21 says, *"Test all things; hold fast what is good."* That is what I have done with God's Word. His Word is proven, tested and it works.

What are some of the damaging thoughts that were brought from Greek philosophy into Christianity that have kept mankind from using his God-given authority? Quoting again from Steve C. Shank's book, Augustine said *"Nothing happens unless the Omnipotent wills it to happen."*[3] This concept mirrors Islam and Hinduism, which teach that you have no control over the things that happen in life. Everything that happens is God's will. Augustine also went on to say a victim *"ought not to attribute* (his suffering) *to the will of men or of angels, or of any created spirit, but rather to His* (God's) *will."*[4]

Augustine's *"extreme sovereignty"* theory took root and became a widespread belief. As previously mentioned, John Calvin taught in *the 1500s that, "all events are governed by God's secret plan."[5] So it's understandable that even modern-day dictionaries and insurance policies define natural disasters as acts of God. But did the early church fathers share this extreme "sovereignty" worldview?* We will take a look at this to see if they embraced this doctrine.

Most reading this book would agree that miracles, healings, signs and wonders are a big part of preaching, teaching, living and proclaiming the full Gospel. These supernatural occurrences throughout the book of Acts and Christianity today draw multitudes to salvation in Christ. Those who embrace the idea that in life, both good and bad things come from God, therefore we are not to question this, rarely see any supernatural miracles, healings, signs and wonders. Much of that belief system breeds passivity, laziness, weakness, physical pain, and suffering supposedly for His glory, and unbelief when it comes to the supernatural power of God. It also breeds a false religious humility, loaded with arrogance and pride. This doctrine embraces everything in this life as the will of God. What happens when things go awry, who gets blamed? God! The attitude is "look at me and how I endure and love this 'angry God' who sends tribulations my way, who is working all things for my good." On the other side of this, some believers think the only way to get miracles, healings, signs and wonders to happen is by manufacturing them. I believe strongly in the grace of God.

Corinna 24 years old! 10 years ago doctors told her spine was like that of an old person. When she received prayer she could feel her spine tighten up and straighten out. Demon manifested and with a big breath she felt her back healed in an instant - **Bitterfeld, Germany June 2015.**

Dustin - 17 years old! Had surgery on left foot, six visible scars, 2 holes not healing. Unable to run or put much pressure on foot! After prayer healed and scars disappear - **Putlitz, Germany April 25, 2018.**

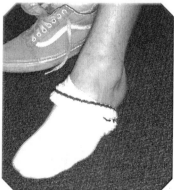

Only had one kidney and was having major problems with it. Received prayer in Jesus' name Friday night after a word of knowledge was given, concerning kidney, in our **Ludwigsburg, Germany November 2016** meeting. Came back the next day to say she was completely healed and all swelling had gone down. Also her waist size shrunk a few inches.

Was deaf in her right ear for 15 years and also had knee problems. After prayer able hear and knee pain gone! **Flensburg, Germany November 2016.**

Ruhollah Rajabali - 31 year old Afghan refugee who recently came to Christ. A look of surprise as Jesus opened his deaf left ear and he could hear clearly - **Ludwigslust, Germany November 20, 2017.**

All the miracles, healings, signs and wonders that take place are because of His grace, but also at the same time, He expects us to press in for these things with faith in Him and not have a passive attitude of "whatever will be will be."

If you want to know more about the *'Negative influence of Greek Philosophy in Western Christianity'* check out chapters 2 and 5 in my book ***OVERCOMING ROADBLOCKS TO HEALING.*** It explains many of the religious traditions that were formed by a belief system founded on Greek philosophy., which was brought into Western Christianity by Augustine and Calvin. Not everything they taught was wrong, but many things were off course because they were looking through the lens of Greek philosophy.

Some might say, "If God is in control, why is there so much poverty, murder, death, famine, and other morbid happenings in the world? Surely if a powerful God is in control He would stop this." Who is in control of the earth, God or mankind? Mankind! God is not to be blamed for the evil things happening on this planet. **Either mankind and or demons are to blame.** For the most part, God will only take control to do good if we give Him the right to! He works through mankind because **He gave earth to mankind!** Many early church leaders taught that if evil is happening on this earth it is because of the choices mankind is making and or evil spirits/fallen angels. Augustine came along around 400AD and contradicted what the Bible and early church leaders taught on this subject.

In order to see just how damaging Augustine's and Calvin's doctrines have been and how far of a departure from the early church their doctrines are, I want to quote from Steve C. Shank's book again. This is from Chapter 3 under the subtitle **Early Church Fathers.** *As we look at the worldview of some of these early church fathers, keep in mind that they lived approximately 250 years before Augustine. Although the earliest church fathers did not hold to the extreme sovereignty view, you will see that they already had to begin refuting such views as early as 100 AD.*

Justin Martyr, AD 100-165: "But the angels transgressed this appointment. . . . They afterward subdued the human race to themselves . . . and among men they sowed murders, wars, adulteries, intemperate deeds, and all wickedness."[6] Notice, however, from Justin's next statement that even back then, around 100 years after Jesus' earth walk, people began to place the blame for all evil upon God: "Where also the poets and mythologists, not knowing that it was the angels and those demons who . . . did these things . . . ascribed them to God Himself."[7]

Clement of Alexandria, AD 150-215, said, "So in no respect is God the author of evil . . . since free choice and inclination originate sins."[8] According to the early church fathers, the tragic and terrible current state of the world is caused by angels and humans misusing their free wills. Jesus instructed us to pray that God's will would be done on earth as it is in heaven (Matthew 6:10). Why would there be a need to pray that if everything that happens on earth was already God's will? This presupposes that God's will is not always being done on earth.

Tertullian, AD 160-220: "Diseases and other grievous calamities are the result of demons whose great business is the ruin of mankind."[9] He further clearly stated, "It is not the part of good and solid faith to refer all things to the will of God."[10] As you can see, this fits the Jesus worldview of 1 John 3:8, "The Son of God appeared for this purpose, to destroy the works of the devil."

Origen, AD 185-254, believed that "evils do not proceed from God.... Famine, blasting of the vine and fruit trees, pestilence among men and beasts: all these are the proper occupations of demons." So, too, demons are "the cause of plagues ... barrenness ... tempests ... and similar calamities."[11] The common belief today is that these are all acts of God. You can clearly see from these and the preceding statements that the early church did not hold to that belief.

Augustine's later doctrines of predestination, all things being the will of God, and his theory of evil always being part of God's mysterious plan for people is a radical departure from Jesus' worldview and that of the earlier church fathers.

It's interesting to note that as you read books and articles from the extreme sovereignty viewpoint, you find very little mention of the devil or demons; Satan is conspicuously missing! Why would there need to be any emphasis upon the evil one if you believed that all things are of God and He's predestined/prearranged everything that happens in life? Extreme sovereignty teaches you to embrace or at least passively accept all events that come your way because they are all part of the sovereign will of God and ultimately serve God's secret plan for your life. As Calvin so clearly explained this viewpoint, "All events are governed by God's secret plan."[12]

If we passively accept the thought that God's will is behind every evil intent and event in life, we mistakenly end up accepting things that are coming at us from Satan as coming from a loving Father God! In doing so, we terribly tarnish the nature of God. We defame His character and open the door for false accusations to be brought against the One who Jesus said is the only One who is perfectly good! (Mark 10:18)

In contrast to this view that teaches "all comes from God, therefore we must embrace it," the Bible actually teaches, Resist the devil, and he will flee from you. (James 4:7, KJV) The Greek word used for resist is loaded with military connotations. As you can see in this rendering, Make war on the Evil One and he will be put to flight before you. (James 4:7, BEV)

If the devil is one of the tools under God's control whose purpose is to work God's will into your life, why would God tell you to resist *him? This makes it clear that we are to receive what's of God and resist what's not! What Satan brings against you does not sovereignly equal God's will for your life. Satan does not love you and have a wonderful plan for your life; neither is he a co-laborer together with God.*

Submit yourselves therefore to God. Resist the devil, and he will flee from you. (James 4:7) It doesn't say submit yourself to all things that come at you in life. Are you submitting yourself to God and resisting the devil, or submitting yourself to the devil and resisting the will of God? "Oh, I'd never do that!" Are you sure? Anything in life that Jesus came to destroy—resist it! Don't submit to what's authored by Satan, thinking that sin, sickness, and all manner of evil will work together for your good.

Because of the miracles Jesus performed, 11,000 people turned to Christ in **Barielly, Uttar Pradesh, India - June 2009.**

Shobha   **Anita**   **Preeti**

Nisha   **Dhamundar**

These five youngsters were all healed of polio by Christ on the closing night of our **Bareilly, India campaign, June 2009.**

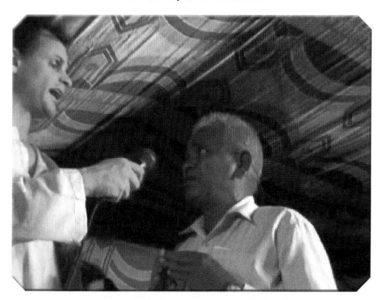

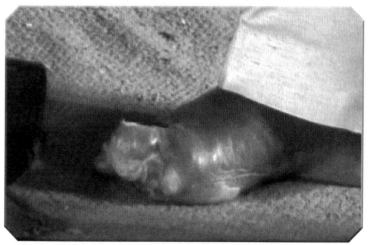

Andrew suffered with diabetes and gangrene. His big toe was eaten away. After mass prayer he was healed and his toe grew back- **Guntur, India February 2001.**

CHAPTER 3

Does God Do Both Good And Evil?

If the earth is in the throes of disaster, **it is not God's fault. It is mankinds!** *Do not be deceived,* my beloved brethren. *Every good gift and every perfect gift is from above,* and comes down from the Father of lights, with whom there is no variation or shadow of turning. (James 1:16-17). This is a simple theology lesson that you would think most Christians would know! God is good and Satan or demons are bad! Satan and God the Father do not work together, nor are they playing on the same team. They are enemies! The earth was given to mankind along with the authority to bring good or evil into this world. Despite possessing this authority, evil men do evil, give place to, have the aid of demon spirits (to carry out evil on the earth), just as Christians have the Holy Spirit/ God (to do good) to carry out their God-given authority. Verse 16 says *Do not be deceived!* Pretty strong warning from James! Yet today so many

37

Christians are deceived thinking God does both good and bad and somehow Satan and God work together to further God's purpose and plan for your life.

We need to realize the earth was given to mankind and if good things are expected then we have to do our part, working in partnership with Holy Spirit, to carry out our authority and bring about good. When we realize we have a part to fulfill and Holy Spirit will work with us to change things then we will cease being beaten up in this life with everything the enemy throws our way. God is not the author of evil occurrences in this world. He gave the earth to mankind to do good or evil. It is man's choice! Many in this world, are being used by the enemy like puppets to carry out evil on the earth. God is not doing this evil, nor is it His will for these things to happen. Much of the evil in this world can be attributed to mankind partnering knowingly or unknowingly with demonic spirits or Satan's will or mankind is to blame for doing bad or stupid things without the aid of demons. Either way mankind makes choices and lives with the consequences of poor choices. This is not God's will.

Those who believe that God orchestrates both good and evil events say everything good or bad (evil) works together for the good of all people in this world. One place they get this is from taking Romans 8:28 out of context; which says, *"and we know that all things work together for good to those who love God, to those who are the called according to His purpose."* Do all things good and bad automatically work together for good, like

Augustine and Calvin believed? It is very important not to pull things out of context to make it adhere to our beliefs. I do not believe all things necessarily work for the good of every person on this planet. The Apostle Paul is not saying in Romans 8:28 that all things good and bad in life are automatically God's will no matter what. Notice how that verse starts, with an 'and'. That means there is something tied to that verse before that. Look at Romans 8:26-27 just before verse 28: *Likewise the Spirit also helps in our weaknesses. For we do not know what we should pray for as we ought, but the Spirit Himself makes intercession for us with groanings which cannot be* **uttered** (Greek says groanings, which can't be uttered in articulate speech or known speech). *Now He who searches the hearts knows what the mind of the Spirit is, because He* **makes intercession for the saints according to the will of God.**

Notice the prior verses are talking about Holy Spirit interceding through us "according to the will of God." He does this when we are praying in the Spirit or tongues, just like Jesus prayed before raising Lazarus from the dead (1 Corinthians 14: 13-15, 18, John 11: 33 & 38). Praying like this is what helps us flow in the power of Holy Spirit especially in an environment where the miracles of Jesus are needed. My testimony of how I was called into ministry revolves around these verses. The purpose of praying in the Spirit is to allow the Holy Spirit to pray through us for God's will to be done. He, Jesus, makes intercession for us (Hebrews 7:25). The Holy Spirit helps us pray according to His will by praying through us in the Spirit or tongues.

1 John 5:14-15 says if we pray for something according to His will: *Now this is the confidence that we have in Him, that* ***if we ask anything according to His will, He hears us.*** *And if we know that He hears us, whatever we ask, we know that* ***we have the petitions that we have asked of Him.*** If the Holy Spirit is praying through us for God's will to be done, don't you think all things will work together for your good? I have seen both good and bad things work together for my good when I have allowed the Holy Spirit to pray through me. There is no such thing as everything just automatically working together for the good of every person on this planet. I could give you hundreds of stories of things not working together for the good of people in this world.

Romans 8:28 also says *to those who are the* ***called according to His purpose.*** Let's say, for example, as a Christian I am not fitting into the purpose and plan that God has for my life. Could things end up not working together for my good? I have seen Christians all over the world, not fitting into God's plan and purpose for their life — they end up living a miserable and defeated life. All things do not work together for good if we understand these verses and live in reality. All things can work together for the good if we are doing what Romans 8:26-28 says to do. **Each person has his or her own free will. Man has a choice. He can yield to God to do good, or be drawn away**

by his own lusts (see James 1:14-15) or yield to demons to do evil.

There is one thing impossible for God to do! That is to tell a lie! *God is not a man, that He should lie, Nor a son of man, that He should repent. Has He said, and will He not do? Or **has He spoken, and will He not make it good*** (Numbers 23:19)? God can't operate or go contrary to His word in Genesis 1:26-28. He holds this universe together by His spoken word. In Psalms 89:34 God says *"My covenant I will not break, **Nor alter the word that has gone out of My lips."*** Hebrews 1:3 says *He is upholding all things by the word of His power.* If God went back on His word this universe would literally collapse because His spoken word holds it together (See Genesis 1). Man was given authority on earth from God. For the most part God has had to operate through mankind's authority, in partnership with him to perform and accomplish great things on this Earth. Jesus, God the Creator in the flesh, was born on this earth, the Son of Man, so He could legally operate in the authority He gave man in the beginning of time. In order to operate in miracles and healings on the earth, He also needed the help and partnership of Holy Spirit (See Acts 10:38).

Every person born on earth has authority, including Jesus Christ, the Creator who was born in the flesh. Hebrews 2:14 Amp says *Therefore, since [these His] children share in flesh and blood [**the physical nature of mankind**], He Himself in a similar manner also **shared in the same [physical nature,***

41

but without sin], so that through [experiencing] death He might make powerless (ineffective, impotent) him who had the power of death—that is, the devil. Greek philosophy made an inroad into the early church. Greek philosophy denies that God could become a man and take on flesh. So many early church leaders warned against this belief and mindset. Here is one of those warnings: *By this you know and recognize the Spirit of God: every spirit that acknowledges and confesses [the fact] that Jesus Christ* (Greek -**the anointed one**) ***has [actually] come in the flesh [as a man]*** *is from God [God is its source]; and every spirit that **does not confess Jesus [acknowledging that He has come in the flesh, but would deny any of the Son's true nature] is not of God;*** *this is the spirit of the antichrist, which you have heard is coming, and is now already in the world* (1 John 4:2-3 AMP) Jesus, the Christ, the anointed one, came in the flesh, stripped Himself of His deity (see Philippians 2:6-7) and came as the SON OF MAN enabling Him to use the **authority (exousia)** God gave man in the beginning of time along with the **power (dunamis)** of the Holy Spirit to destroy the works of the devil.

Greek philosophy could not comprehend God becoming a man, but that is exactly what Jesus the Christ, God the Creator did! He took on flesh and blood. John warned the early church about this false doctrine that stated God did not come in the flesh. Greek philosophy states this was not possible. Mark 10:27 says *But Jesus looked at them and said, "With men it is impossible, but not with God; for with God all things are possible."* It's not impossible for God to humble Himself and take on flesh. He did that of His own free will. He came, walked, lived, and was tortured and put to death by His own creation, all to redeem mankind and to regain our authority.

In Greek philosophy, with the Greek gods and many other religions they put most of the emphasis on the spiritual realm and the gods that dwell there. In these religions of man the emphasis is always how big, powerful and out of touch God or these gods are with mankind. That is why the Greeks during Jesus' time had a very hard time believing God the Creator humbled Himself and came to **earth in the FLESH, a man.** They could not wrap their minds around that. Greek philosophy separates the spiritual and physical realms. This teaching has been brought right into our present day Western Christianity. The over emphasis was always on the spiritual and man becoming more spiritual. Greek Gnosticism was all about separating the spiritual and physical realms unlike what the Jews and Jesus taught. Spiritual gnostics are mostly focused on the spiritual realm and try to stay disconnected from the physical realm. This is a big part of what Augustine taught. Their teachings and belief system were based on becoming more spiritual in order to be more disconnected from the physical realm.

An agnostic is someone who is only in touch with the physical realm and very disconnected from the spiritual realm and God. They believe there might be a God and then again there might not be a God but that does not matter to them because they are so focused on the physical realm and are totally disconnected from God. But our God, who is a Spirit, (see John 4:24) invaded the physical realm, and became flesh to get on our level, so He could have relationship with us, not religion. One reason He came was to bridge the great divide between man and God and the spiritual and physical realms, but also to have authority on the earth and get back our authority which had been lost to Satan.

This song *How many Kings* by **Downhere** sums up what our great God, Jesus Christ did for mankind:

Is this who we've waited for?
'Cause how many kings stepped down from their thrones
How many lords have abandoned their homes?
How many greats have become the least for me?
And how many gods have poured out their hearts
To romance a world that is torn all apart
How many fathers gave up their sons for me?
...ONLY ONE DID THAT FOR ME."

Masses turn to Christ in **Sofia, Rochovsky** and other cities in **Bulgaria September 1991**, right after the Iron Curtain falls.

Rafael Valverde - Hit by bull. He had many broken ribs above his sternum. He came to the outreach drunk, cursing God and us. During mass prayer he was instantly healed and sobered up. He went home and slept all through the night with no pain for the first time since the bull had hit him. Came back the next night and accepted Jesus and demonstrated his miracle - **Parrita, Costa Rica April 1991.**

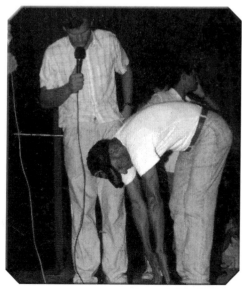

CHAPTER 4

Full Of Compassion And Slow To Anger

We were the reason that He gave His life. We were the reason that He suffered and died. To a world that was lost, He gave all He could give to show us a reason to live (words and music by David Meece Album Are You Ready)

Unlike the Greek god Zeus (god of thunder) our God is not full of wrath and anger, ready to beat up His own. Instead of raising His hands to strike and destroy He spread out His arms in love to hang on a cross, suffer, bleed and die a horrible death. We were the reason He suffered and died. Jesus summed it all up: *Greater love has no one than this, than to lay down one's life for his friends* (John 15:13). He desires our friendship and fellowship.

Psalms 145:8-9 says *The Lord is gracious and **full of compassion, Slow to anger** and **great in mercy**. The Lord is **good*** *to all, And His tender mercies are over all His works.* He is not like Zeus, or the gods of other religions of men. God is not like the religious traditions of men, that have been greatly influenced by Greek philosophy. They have depicted Him as a schizophrenic God who does both good and evil to mankind. In reality, He is overflowing with compassion and so very slow to anger. He does not work with Satan and demons to carry out evil, to steal, kill or destroy life. Jesus is not like Augustine portrayed Him to be. He is not working with Satan, who is a thief. *The thief does not come except to steal, and to kill, and to destroy. I have come that they may have life, and that they may have it more abundantly* (John 10:10). Satan and demons do bad but Jesus came to do good and give us abundant life.

During September 2017 the USA experienced major hurricanes, one after another, causing much death, flooding and destruction. Christian leaders who were influenced by Greek philosophy or Calvinism said "this is the wrath of God on the USA. God is judging the USA for its sin and evil actions." By the way we do not worship Zeus, we worship Jesus, who showed us what the Heavenly Father is truly like (see John 14:9). Greek philosophy has greatly distorted many Christians view of the Heavenly Father. I greatly disagreed with this distorted view of the heavenly Father. I wrote on my Facebook wall that we have authority over these demonic storms sent to steal, kill and destroy life. Many people agreed with me and we began to pray and take authority over Hurricane Irma as it was heading to the Florida coasts.

Hurricane Irma was causing major destruction on the islands in its path as it moved towards Florida. It a was a category 5 hurricane, the worst ever, with winds up to 185mph! A day after sharing my views on Facebook and asking people to pray and take authority over this demonic storm I had a dream that it reached the Florida coast and was immediately reduced to a category 2 hurricane. I shared this on Facebook and rallied more prayer support for Florida. All the weather forecasters said it will hit Florida as a category 5 hurricane and cause major destruction. Florida was preparing for the worst! It hit the Florida Keys as a catagory 5 hurricane but the next day as soon as it reached the Florida mainland it immediately went from a catagory 5 to a catagory 2 hurricane, to the shock of the weather forecasters.

I have seen major storms and tornadoes change course when we have taken authority in Jesus' name. Jesus said *"peace be still"* to a storm and the waves ceased (see Mark 35-39). The origin of the storm was not from God. So He took authority over this demonic storm that was trying to take them out. The Body of Christ needs to rise up and understand the authority that was given to us by God in the beginning. What a gift we have been given from heaven! Let's use it!

By the way, if God is judging the USA by sending natural disasters on it, then why did He not judge Israel and Rome at the time He walked this earth in the flesh? History shows very clearly how very evil and wicked the religious leaders of Jesus day were and even more how perverted and evil the Romans were. If this is what God does, He must be extremely busy running around the world destroying the earth with all the natural disasters that are taking place all over the world. How absurd to believe this!

Look at Jesus' reaction to the disciples when they thought Jesus needed to send fire and destroy some people who ignored Him. *Now it came to pass, when the time had come for Him to be received up, that He steadfastly set His face to go to Jerusalem, and sent messengers before His face. And as they went, they entered a village of the Samaritans, to prepare for Him. But they did not receive Him, because His face was set for the journey to Jerusalem. And when His disciples James and John saw this, they said, "Lord, do You want us to command fire to come down from heaven and consume them, just as Elijah did?" But* **He turned and rebuked them,** *and said,* **"You do not know what manner of spirit you are of. For the Son of Man did not come to destroy men's lives but to save them."** *And they went to another village* (Luke 9:51-56). This Samaritan village refused to receive Christ. James and John (the sons of thunder) wanted to call fire down from heaven and consume them. I wonder if they were just a little bit influenced by Greek philosophy and the Greek god Zeus, a teaching that was spreading around at that time? Jesus rebuked them and said *"You do not know what manner or spirit you are of. For the son of Man did not come to destroy men's lives but to save them"* (Luke 9:55-56). They were operating by the same religious spirit that drove the Pharisees and Sadducees. Today we have many in Christian circles operating by that same spirit. A big reason for this is the influence of Greek philosophy here in Western Christianity passed down by religious traditions of man. God's heart is for restoration and love.

Many Christians are sidetracked and constantly talking about the judgment of God or how God will be pouring out his wrath on countries because of all the sin. They need to keep things in perspective. God the Father did judge our sin. It was judged 2,000 years ago at Calvary as His only Son hung suspended, bleeding and dying between heaven and earth to pay the price of our sin. *For He made Him who knew no sin to be sin for us, that we might become the righteousness of God in Him* (2 Corinthians 5:21). His wrath was poured out at Calvary. Now we operate under His grace and righteousness. We get good things from Him we do not deserve and things we could never earn through our own good deeds.

We no longer live in the time of the Old Testament prophets who spoke of the judgement and wrath of God. We are not living in the time of the book of Revelation where God is pouring out His wrath. Our God went to the cross and took the judgement and the wrath on Himself. We live in the dispensation of the grace of God. We need to live our lives on the right side of Calvary not before Calvary. Our God, Jesus Christ is so good. He took our punishment at Calvary so we can experience His love, mercy, grace, healing, deliverance and so much more. Romans 2:4 (Amp) says *Or do you have no regard for the **wealth of His kindness and tolerance and patience [in withholding His wrath]**? Are you [actually] unaware or ignorant [of the fact] that **God's kindness leads you to repentance** [that is, to change your inner self, your old way of thinking—seek His purpose for your life]?*

If you study the time Jesus walked this earth perversion, corruption and sin were running rampant. All you have to do is study a little history from that time. Bill O'Reilly's book **Killing Jesus** is a great book to read of the history of that time. Yet Jesus said *For God so loved the world that He gave His only begotten Son, that whoever believes in Him should not perish but have everlasting life. For God **did not send His Son into the world to condemn the world,** but that **the world through Him might be saved*** (John 3:16-17). If there ever were people who deserved the judgement and wrath of God, the Romans and Jewish religious leaders of that time deserved it! Instead, they had the Creator of the universe come down in love to serve and to lay down His life as a ransom and absorb the judgement and wrath of God for us. Jesus said *"Just as the Son of Man did not come to be served, but to serve, and to give His life a ransom for many"* (Matthew 20:28).

Severe Storm Rebuked In Jesus Name- Bamba, Kenya

During the Winter of 1988 I had the privilege of traveling with Peter Youngren and a team of mostly Canadians to Kenya, Africa. I took a small team and ministered in the rural village of Bamba, Kenya. This village had about 10,000 people who lived within a five mile radius. I conducted a four day open air outreach there. Altogether about 2,400 Kenyans gave their hearts to Christ in this outreach. Many manifested with demons and were set free during this outreach. One 13 year old girl, Kathuma Baya, was born with a club foot. As we prayed a mass prayer taking authority over sickness and infirmities the crowd began screaming as many of them watched Holy Spirit make her club foot straight. Many

Kathuma (r) - was born with a clubfoot. During mass prayer the crowd started screaming as many of them watched Holy Spirit straighten out her foot right in front of their eyes- **Bamba, Kenya 1988.**

crippled, deaf and blind people were also healed those four days.

By the third day of the outreach the momentum was building and there was excitement for the evening outreach. During the early afternoon Jerry Jameson and Hazel Hill taught the leaders. During Hazel's teaching it was bright and sunny, but thick black storm clouds started gathering from every direction and completely darkened the sky over the village. Soon there was a heavy downpour and it looked like we would have to cancel our outreach. I realized this was demonic.

As the heavy rain and wind continued, I went up to the stage and announced through the sound system (so the whole village could hear), that as proof that Jesus is alive He would take control of the weather and not a drop of rain would fall from 4pm the time our open air outreach started onwards. People in this village probably thought I was nuts. Nothing changed immediately but by 4pm the rain completely ceased. We watched as a strong wind came in, clouds blew in every direction and a bright sunny sky broke through in Bamba. We have experienced similar miracles in India and Nepal on multiple occasions, where Jesus has intervened and completely stilled the storm so that our outreaches could continue uninterrupted.

That night was powerful. About 1,000 received Christ. One young man with polio, who had never walked, had come scooting himself along using his arms to attend the teaching time. His legs were just skin and bones and when the rain fell he was left kneeling in a mud puddle. He was filled with Holy Spirit during the teaching time. During the outreach when we prayed a mass prayer for the crowd he stood up and walked for the first time in his life right up to the stage. He then had to sit down because his legs had no muscle.

On the final night of this outreach nearly 3,000 people gathered. While praying a mass healing prayer for the crowd many were instantly healed by Holy Spirit. The first five people that came up to the stage had been blind, but now could see. Kadzo Ndoko was blind, deaf and mute and after prayer was instantly healed by Jesus. She was able to demonstrate that she could see, hear and repeat words spoken! Miracles, healings, signs and wonders draw people to our loving Jesus. Rebuking that storm in Jesus' name and seeing what heaven did was great and inspiring. It ignited faith in that place.

Partnering With Demons

On April 25, 2015 a devastating earthquake hit Nepal. Nearly 9,000 people were killed and 22,000 injured. It was the worst natural disaster to hit Nepal since the 1934 Nepal-Bihar earthquake. The epicenter was 50 miles northwest of the Kathmandu, the capital of Nepal. There were many aftershocks. The earthquake even triggered an avalanche many miles away on Mount Everest, killing 21 and making that the deadliest day on the mountain in history. Hundreds of thousands of people were rendered homeless and entire villages were flattened. On top of all this destruction, it was reported that survivors were preyed upon by human traffickers who were involved in the supply of girls and women to the brothels of South Asia. These traffickers took advantage of the chaos to prey on the girls and women who had lost their homes in the earthquake.[1] Those of the extreme sovereignty viewpoint would say this was part of God's sovereign plan and all things work for the good (perversion of Romans 8:28 which we addressed earlier). Is that true and scriptural or just religious tradition that was passed down by Western Church leaders influenced Greek philosophy when it merged with Christianity in 400AD?

Let's look at this from the viewpoint that God gave this earth to mankind like we read in Genesis 1:26-28 and Psalm 115:16, and that mankind is responsible for how he uses his authority, whether for good or evil. Depending on how mankind uses his authority, there are good or bad consequences. Could it be that mankind is somewhat responsible for this destruction in Nepal? Let's see!

For the past 260 plus years there is celebration and animal sacrifice that takes place at the Gadhimai Temple of Bariyarpur, in the Bara District about 100 miles south of Kathmandu, by the Indo-Nepal border. It is primarily celebrated by the Madheshi and Bihari people. It is actually the largest animal sacrifice in the entire world. In recent years it is conducted every five years. The most recent being November 28, 2014! Less than 5 months before the devastating Nepal earthquake on April 25, 2015!

The purpose of this festival is to appease the Hindu goddess Gadhimai, the goddess of power. This goddess (demon) appeared 260 years ago to the man who started this festival of animal sacrifice. This demon asked for five humans to be sacrificed but he did not want to offer humans so animals were offered instead. Participants **believe that animal sacrifices to the Hindu goddess Gadhimai will end evil and bring prosperity.**

It is estimated that **250,000 animals were sacrificed during the Gadhimai Festival of 2009.** The ritual killings were performed by more than 200 men in a concrete slaughterhouse near

Water buffaloes slaughtered and sacrificed to Hindu goddess Ghadimai in 2009!

the temple. Millions of Hindus attend this sacrifice. The area around the Gadhimai Temple had animals piled up for a 2 to 3 mile radius. In 2009 more than 20,000 male water buffaloes were beheaded to this goddess Gadhimai not to mention all the other animals sacrificed. [2]

Jesus said *The thief does not* **come except to steal, and to kill, and to destroy.** *I have come that they* **may have life,** *and that they may have it more abundantly* (John 10:10). Spending much of my time in ministry in India (since 1986) and Nepal (since 1991), I work mostly among Hindus and Muslims. Hindus are said to worship over 33 million gods. Jesus perfectly describes the three main gods of Hinduism in John 10:10. **Krishna**, who history tells us was a **thief, Kali** the **goddess of death** and **Shiva** the **god of destruction.** You do not have to travel far in India or Nepal to see temples and shrines to these three main gods of the Hindu religion. What I have noticed about Hindus is they do not worship their gods so much because they are in love with these gods, but because they fear these gods. Many powerful Hindu leaders in these countries use that belief, superstition and fear to control the masses in the direction they want to take the country.

Jesus described what Satan and demons do: they steal, kill and destroy! Jesus said *"I have come that they* **may have life,** *and that they may have it more abundantly."* Sadly, in the extreme sovereignty belief, God is labeled as the one who does the evil and bad things on earth and there is very little mention of Satan and demons and what they do, just like in the book of Job. Job thought it was God who was afflicting him and doing all the evil against him (see Job 1:21, 13:24, and 16:9). The book of Job was written 155 years before Moses. Job had no idea that there was a Satan or demons that afflicted him. *So **Satan** departed from the presence of the Lord and **struck Job with loathsome boils** and agonizingly painful sores from the sole of his foot to the crown of his head* (Job 2:7 Amp). Job had to have his poor theology corrected by God. God said to Job *"Will you condemn Me [your God] that you may [appear to] be righteous and justified?"* (Job 40:8 Amp). The neat thing about Job is he humbled himself, repented, and God restored twice as much to Job after his 9 month ordeal (see Job 42:10).

Could it be that the goddess Gadhimai is actually a demon that has come to steal, kill and destroy, and that mankind has partnered with it for centuries? Could it be that the blood sacrifice to Gadhimai on November 28, 2014 brought death and destruction to Nepal in April 25, 2015? Did sacrificing to Ghadimai give demons legal right to steal, kill and destroy life? Could it be this was not the God we worship causing such destruction? That is what I believe! Those that sacrificed the many thousands of animals to this bloodthirsty demon prayed to this demon to end evil and bring prosperity. Instead on April 25, 2015 they reaped destruction, death, poverty, sorrow, misery and horrific evil in Nepal.

Pray for these people as they have not heard of the love and sacrifice of Jesus and do not know any better than to partner with demons. Our goal is to reach them to say there is better way. You do not have to appease Jesus, God the Creator. He has purchased and paid the price for salvation for all mankind. Salvation is a gift from Him. All you have to do is receive Him as Lord, Savior, Healer, Deliverer and receive the gift of eternal life **He purchased with His blood sacrifice 2,000 years ago** when He took on flesh and was born on earth. He is full of compassion, mercy and slow to anger and longs for friendship and relationship with mankind. *For the wages of sin is death, but the gift of God is eternal life in Christ Jesus our Lord* (Romans 6:23). We do not have to work for or earn this gift. Just receive it with simple faith and trust in Him.

There are consequences for using our God-given authority on earth to partner with evil spirits just like Adam did when he yielded to his flesh, submitted to the lies of Satan in the beginning of time and lost his God-given authority to Satan. *Do not be deceived, God is not mocked [He will not allow Himself to be ridiculed, nor treated with contempt nor allow His precepts to be scornfully set aside]; for **whatever a man sows,** this and **this only is what he will reap.** For the one who sows to his flesh [his sinful capacity, his worldliness, his disgraceful impulses] **will reap from the flesh ruin and destruction,** but the one who sows to the Spirit will from the Spirit reap eternal life* (Galatians 6:7-8 Amp).

Please notice how it says there is a reaping that will bring ruin and destruction but it does not say God brings this ruin and destruction. Mankind brings it on himself with wrong choices of his own freewill and when he does evil or knowingly or unknowingly uses his authority to partner with demons.

So many undeniable miracles by Jesus! About 3,800 attend last day of **Sukhar, Nepal** outreach. Around 4,300 came to Christ during this 3-day outreach. - **February 2014.**

5,500 turn to Christ in a 3 day open air outreach in **Surkhet, Nepal October 2016.**

Harikala Basel - Deafmute 50 years. Speaks & hears clearly . Daughter confirms healing. Many deaf and mute were healed in this outreach! They could hear and speak - **Surkhet, Nepal Oct 2016.**

Nirmala - Could not walk for 2 months or speak for many years. Demonstrates she is healed! Progressive healing from 1st day onward - **Surkhet, Nepal Oct 2016 .**

Broken wrist healed! Had much pain. Demonstrates wrist is healed - **Surkhet, Nepal Oct 2016.**

CHAPTER 5

Mirror Imaging

He said to them, *"But who do you say that I am?"* Simon *Peter answered and said, "**You are the Christ, the Son of the living God.**" Jesus answered and said to him, "Blessed are you, Simon Bar-Jonah, for **flesh and blood has not revealed this to you,** but My Father who is in heaven. And I also say to you that you are Peter, and on **this rock I will build My church, and the gates of Hades shall not prevail against it*** (Matthew 16:15-18). Jesus did not build His Church upon Peter, but He built it on what Peter stated by revelation knowledge from Heaven. Jesus said that He will build His Church on the rock of revelation knowledge that He is the Christ. Notice also He said the **gates (Greek-authority, influence and leadership)** of Hades (Hell) shall not prevail against that rock and against His Church, the Body of Christ.

In Matthew 16:19 (Amp) Jesus says, *I will give you the keys (authority) of the kingdom of heaven; and whatever you bind [forbid, declare to be improper and unlawful] on earth will have [already] been bound in heaven, and whatever you loose [permit, declare lawful] on earth will have [already] been loosed in heaven."* If negative things are happening on earth, believers have the authority to bring about positive change. In this verse Jesus is talking about changing the spiritual atmosphere to see permanent change in the physical realm. One thing taught in Greek philosophy and promoted by Augustine is that **the spiritual realm has preeminence over the physical realm.** This is most certainly true! But Jesus, the Jews, and the early church did not separate the spiritual and physical realms as taught by Plato and those who embrace Greek philosophy. If we can affect the spiritual realm we can see numerous miracles or circumstances change for the better in the physical realm. Spirit filled Christians have the authority and the power of Holy Spirit to change the spiritual realm and then, in turn, to change the physical realm and the circumstances around them. Jesus gave us the keys of the kingdom of heaven. If you have the keys of a kingdom, everything in that kingdom is at your disposal. Heaven is the main kingdom of the entire universe. Jesus wants us to use the keys of the kingdom of Heaven (here on earth).

Some of what Jesus talks about here in Matthew 16:19, is based on the concept of *mirror imaging.* This refers to affecting the spiritual realm for success in the physical realm.

You might say mirror imaging, what is that? It might be hard for men to understand this principle, but not women. Women go into the bathroom in the morning and get in front of a mirror and a short time later come out transformed. Why? Because they look at that reflection of themselves in the mirror and fix whatever they need to beautify themselves. Most men hardly know what a mirror is. This is what Jesus is talking about. Reflecting heaven unto this earth. Jesus said pray like this *"Your will be done On earth as it is in heaven"* (Matthew 6:10). Is there any sickness, infirmities, demonic torment, wars, hurricanes, killings, or hatred in heaven? No! Then we should be reflecting, like a mirror, heaven unto this earth.

I personally believe for the most part everything that happens in the physical realm, such as miracles or a move of the Holy Spirit came as a result of affecting the spiritual realm first. We need to affect the spiritual realm to see results in the physical realm. We need to reflect heaven on the Earth, just like a reflection in a mirror. The Israelites understood this concept and were in tune to the spiritual realm. They knew that if they could affect the spiritual realm they would see great success in the physical realm.

2 Chronicles 20 is a good example of this 'Mirror Imaging' principle, found throughout the Old Testament. The people

Jesus ministered to understood this principle because they were in tune to both the spiritual and physical realms. They did not separate the spiritual and physical realms like we are taught here in the West to believe because of the influence of Greek philosophy. Judah called upon the living God with fasting and prayer to affect the spiritual and the natural realm. King Jehoshaphat also did this when the combined armies of Moab, Ammon and others besieged Judah and there appeared no way out for Judah (Ref. 2 Chronicles 20:1-30). They were greatly outnumbered!

After praying, fasting, operating in faith and affecting the spiritual realm God spoke through a prophet in 2 Chronicles 20:15, *"And he said, Listen, all you of Judah and you inhabitants of Jerusalem, and you, King Jehoshaphat! Thus says the Lord to you: Do not be afraid nor dismayed because of this great multitude, for **the battle is not yours, but God's**."* King Jehoshaphat understood that God would deliver Judah from the vast enemy army and instead of sending soldiers out to face the enemy, he sent the praise and worship teams to worship God before the enemy. Worship is powerful in affecting the spiritual realm. As they were praising God, the Lord sent ambushments (angels) against the enemy, and the enemy was defeated. These kind of events happened time and time again in the Old Testament when the spiritual realm was affected, allowing great things to happen in the physical realm.

Angels Move On Our Behalf

In Isaiah 37:36 the Lord sent one angel who killed 185,000 Assyrians, once again protecting Judah from the enemy. King Hezekiah prayed to the Lord, affecting the spiritual realm, and then saw results in the physical realm. Many nominal Christians think angels are just fat little naked babies as portrayed on glass-stained windows. I guarantee you a fat little naked baby could not kill 185,000 people. Angels are powerful! Hebrews 1:14 says, *Are they not all ministering spirits sent forth to minister for those who will inherit salvation?*

Angels move on our behalf when we affect the spiritual realm and stand on the authority of God's Word. *Bless the Lord, you His angels,* ***Who excel in strength, who do His word, heeding the voice of His word.*** *Bless the Lord, all you His hosts, You ministers of His, who do His pleasure* (Psalms 103:20-21). Angels excel in strength and heed the voice of His word. There is tremendous authority released when we stand on, confess and live by His Word. All heaven backs up His Word.

Jesus said in Luke 12:8-9 *"Also I say unto you, whoever confesses Me before men, Him the Son of Man will* ***confess before the angels of God.*** *But He who denies Me before men will be denied before the angels of God."* When we are confessing Christ before men we are setting a spiritual force into motion. God's angels are going out to minister to the heirs of salvation.

The Babylonians understood and acted upon this principle of mirror image as well. The difference lay in the fact that they called upon demonic powers for victory. They built a city and buried it underground. Then they built the replica of that city above the ground in order to call upon the powers of the underworld. They affected the spiritual realm and as a result won great battles and conquered many in the physical realm, in their time. Assembly of God Pastor Don Brokus from Cody, Wyoming shared this with me regarding mirror imaging. *"**Mirror image** is an old concept understood in many ancient cultures, e.g., Sumerian, Babylonian and Hebrew. Sumerian and Babylonian foundation prayer cones or spikes have been excavated and translated, and the purpose of those cones were to "appease" the underworld gods (they were placed at the corners of the underworld city and buried). Pagan gods are not, nor ever were, viewed as benevolent."*

Do Jesus or The Bible Teach Natural/ Spiritual Division?

Let's take a look at what Jesus and the Bible have to say about the natural/spiritual division. We will see clearly through the scriptures that the ancient Jews and Jesus did not divide these two realms, but operated with both the spiritual and natural or invisible and visible realms being fully integrated or as one. This is important to understand if you want to see heaven invade this earth with Christ's miracles, healings, signs and wonders.

I believe Jesus had perfect theology. You can't have better

theology than what He taught. In John 14:9 Jesus said, *He who has seen Me has seen the Father.* He also said in John 6:38, *"For I have come down from heaven, not to do My own will, but the will of Him who sent Me."* John 1:14 says, *And the Word became flesh and dwelt among us...* I do not think you can get better theology than Jesus, the Living Word made manifest. As followers of Christ, we need to **filter all our theology through Jesus and what He accomplished at Calvary.** It is important as believers to live our lives on the right side of the cross. Many Christians live their life as if Jesus never went to the cross. We are living under a New Covenant, which is much better than any previous covenant because Jesus laid down His life and was raised from the dead.

What we are basically doing according to this principal of mirror imaging in Matthew 16:19 is reflecting heaven onto the earth by not separating the spiritual and natural or invisible and visible realms. With the keys Jesus gave us, we can use our authority in the physical realm to affect the spiritual realm and then see the manifestation of that in the physical realm. For Jesus there was no separating these two realms, they are both one and fully integrated. That is why Jesus prayed in Matthew 6:10, *"Your kingdom come. Your will be done on **earth*** (physical realm) *as it is in **heaven*** (spiritual realm)."* We are to reflect God's Kingdom here on planet Earth. Why would Jesus pray your will be done if, like Augustine and Calvin believed, everything good and bad that happens in life is God's will? It is clear there are many things happening on this earth that are not God's will. That is why Jesus came to do the will of the Father (John 6:38) and destroy the works (will) of the devil (see 1 John 3:8).

Paul said, *For we walk by faith, not by sight* (2 Corinthians 5:7). Many in Christian circles are doing everything they can in the natural or physical realm to bring about the answers to their prayers. Their faith is totally dependent on what can be worked up in the natural realm, what they feel, see, hear, etc. Faith in God moves beyond the physical realm or what can be achieved in the physical realm into affecting the spiritual realm and bringing the manifestation into the physical realm.

Hebrews 11:1-3 says, *Now faith is the substance of things hoped for, the evidence of things not seen. For by it the elders obtained a good testimony. By faith we understand that the worlds were framed by the word of God, so that the things which are seen were not made of things which are visible.* Faith can actually bring about something (physical) out of nothing (invisible). Faith activates the miracle working power of God the same way fear activates Satan's destructive power. Rather than releasing authority into Satan's and demons will through fear and worry release your authority through faith in what God has said in His Word.

Fear and worry not only activate Satan or demonic power just like faith activates God's creative power but it gives Satan and demons authority to operate in our lives and the world around us. Look at Job! *For the thing I greatly feared has come upon me, And what I dreaded has happened to me* (Job 3:25). Even though Job's heart was right before God and he had limited knowledge of what was happening to him, could fear have allowed the door to be open for Satan to afflict Job (see Job 2:17)? The Hebrew actually states I feared a fear and it came upon me. It has been said that the words 'fear not' are mentioned in the Bible 365 times. That is one for each day of the year. Fear is faith perverted. Faith needs to be the center of our decision making process. Do not let fears and phobias from the past control your future destiny. It is putting faith in what the Devil has said about your circumstances. Put faith in God's word not what the Devil, demons or your physical circumstances dictate.

Some people do not even realize they are living their lives in fear. Let me explain. They let negative experiences from the past dictate how their lives should be lived today. They do not appear to be living in fear outwardly, but by their subconscious actions and decisions they show that they are living in fear. It can greatly impact the lives of those that are close to them by passing on those fears and phobias. Fear is contagious just like faith is contagious. Fear gives Satan and demons authority to bring harm into our life.

In chapter 14 of his book, author Steve C. Shank shares: *It's been said, "Fear is always built on a lie—deal with the lie, and fear will die!" You deal with the lie by replacing it with God's Truth— what has God said about this situation? God's Word brings faith with it; when faith comes in, fear goes out! Fear cannot abide or dwell in the environment of the Truth. You eliminate fear's environment by dwelling in the environment of the Truth. Faith is always built on the Truth—live in the Truth, and you're fear-proof.*

John 8:31-32 says, *Then Jesus said to those Jews who believed Him, "If you **abide** (Greek- continue) in My word, you are My disciples indeed. And you shall know the truth, and the truth shall make you free."* It is one thing to know scriptures like many Christians do and quite another thing to continue in the Word, to know and experience the Word working in your life. Many Christians know the truth of God's Word but are still bound. Mental assent to the Word of God will not cut it. The Bible is spiritual truth. If someone is sick or diseased the fact is they are sick or diseased. This is not "mind over matter" or "ignore it and it will go away." Jesus did not tell us to ignore the mountain but to face the mountain and speak to it with authority and in faith believing that it would be removed (Mark 11:22-23). Pastor Bill Johnson says, *"Faith doesn't deny a problem's existence. It denies it a place of influence."* The mountain before you is the truth (fact) in the physical realm. Here is the difference with those who do not separate the two realms, as in Greek philosophy. You can take spiritual truth (the Word of God) which supersedes physical facts and apply it with faith and watch the spiritual truth do away with the physical facts (physical realm truth) by creating something (physical) out of nothing (invisible). That is how faith in God's Word works. It's a whole lot of fun watching God come through!

In August 2007 **Randy Clark** prayed for impartation over me in Castle Rock, Colorado. I did not feel anything but received it by faith. Prior to this prayer for impartation we were already seeing many mighty miracles in our outreaches around the world. But things quickly were taken to a whole new level after receiving this prayer for impartation. A short time later our daughter Charisma and her friend saw an angel two stories tall walking through our home.

My first time hearing Randy Clark and Bill Johnson speak was at my former home church in Castle Rock, Colorado August 2007. More than 1,000 recorded healings took place in that conference. I received prayer for impartation from Randy and ever since then Jesus and angels have been appearing in many of our outreaches in northern India. During one of the nights in Castle Rock someone took this photo of an angel appearing in the meeting.

A short time after that we left for India. Sharmila will share with you what transpired there and has now become a regular occurrence in our outreaches in Northern India ever since 2007.

Hindus & Muslims See & Hear Jesus!

Fall 2007 Report by Sharmila Anderson

"Many times I find it extremely difficult to express in words the power, compassion and mercy of Jesus Christ. Our outreach in **Moradabad, India** *was one such time. I will to try my best to describe what happened there as Jesus tangibly revealed Himself to many Hindus and Muslims. Prior to our departure for this outreach Mark had mentioned that he sensed that this trip would be a turning point for the ministry in India, that something powerful was about to break forth!*

We conducted a 5-day city wide, open-air campaign in Moradabad October 23- 27, 2007. During this period approximately 11,500 people decided to become Jesus' followers, by surrendering to His Lordship, and many hundreds were healed of all kinds of ailments. Many of the people who testified of being healed said they either audibly heard Jesus' voice, or saw Him face to face, or saw angels. One gentleman said he saw thousands of angels all over the campaign grounds.

From the first night we knew that Holy Spirit was pouring Himself out on hungry Hindus and Muslims, as many testified of being healed. Most did not get the opportunity to testify of their healing as it was getting very late and the meeting had to be closed down. By the final night, over 9,000 people had gathered, hungry to hear about Jesus. Many of them for the first time in their life.

On the first night **Mukesh Kumar** *testified that during prayer* for healing he told Jesus "if you are real I want to experience you." Immediately he felt warmth in his body followed by coolness, and then a strong current went through him, after which he was fell to the ground. He arose knowing that Jesus was the true God and decided to follow Him. **Momine**, a young Muslim boy had no blood circulation on one side of his face, as a result of which he could not blink his eye. The Lord touched him and he was able to blink his eye and speak clearly.

Vandana sat alone at the far end of the grounds. When we had people come forward for mass healing prayer she remained sitting alone in the darkness. She suffered with seizures, asthma and was mentally tormented. During the mass healing prayer she saw someone walk towards her from the crowd. It was Jesus. He walked up to her, touched her, told her that that everything will be OK and she was healed. **Sunil Massih** saw Jesus in the midst of the crowd along with thousands of angels. He said that one of the angels touched him.

Vineet Kumar, 12 years old, suffered with severe pain in his lungs. He testified that someone touched him and he heard an audible voice say to him, "son you are healed! Go up and testify." This young boy was extremely charged. He began to boldly praise Jesus in front of the huge crowd.

These are just a few of the healings that occurred. The blind saw, the deaf heard, cripples danced for joy, tumors dissolved, the demonized were set free, and individuals on their death beds were *healed.* THE POWER OF GOD WAS PRESENT TO HEAL. *Many people testified that they literally* **felt a presence reach into their bodies, pull the sickness out of them or put body parts back in place.**

Neelam - *Was dying. She suffered with jaundice (swollen liver) and was bedridden. Jesus walked through her bedroom walls and appeared to her. He reached over and caressed her in bed, telling her to go the campaign and she would be healed! She came out to the campaign. After prayer she testified of her miraculous healing! It is really a good meeting when you have Jesus going door to door telling people to attend the meeting because He would be showing up to heal many! You can't work up that kind of scenario. It's totally a grace thing.*

The news of the campaign spread to surrounding towns and by the final night people had come from great distances to receive healing from Christ. The local television station covered the campaign, which was good publicity for us. Articles about the campaign, Jesus healing people and Mark's message appeared in newspapers too.

We have heard that on the Sunday after the campaign each church added an average of 5-6 new families. Healing testimonies continue to flow in. The pastors are determined to disciple all the souls harvested during this campaign. The media in Moradabad said that "THE TRUE GOD HAS VISITED OUR CITY AND HAS SHAKEN IT!"

When the prayer of impartation is prayed over individuals an authority to perform miracles and healings often take place or as in my case that anointing was taken to another level. The Apostle Paul says 2 Timothy 1:6 says *Therefore I remind you to stir up the gift of God which is in you through the laying on of my hands.* He also said *For I long to see you, that I may impart to you some spiritual gift, so that you may be established* (Romans 1:11). Praying over one another for impartation was a regular practice of the early church.

Randy Clark teaching leaders in **Chandigarh, India January 2011.** A number of people have been raised from the dead and many powerful miracles have taken place since Randy prayed over these leaders for impartation.

As far as someone who operates in a strong anointing for impartation, I would highly recommend attending a **Randy Clark** conference. In all my travels around the world, for many years, I have not seen anyone that Holy Spirit has so strongly anointed for this purpose of praying over people for impartation. We brought Randy Clark into India in January 2011 to train leaders we work with. The fruit from that conference was outstanding! Miracles, healings, signs, and wonders became a regular occurrence with many of the leaders who attended and we now work with on a regular basis. It has spread out to many other leaders in India. Some of these Indian leaders have also seen the dead raised since attending that conference.

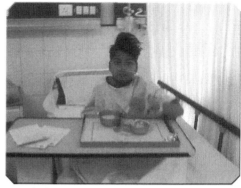

Lakshay was raised from dead right after the Chandigarh, India Randy Clark Conference. Here is a photo of him right after being raised from the dead - **Delhi, India 2011.**

Lakshay was raised from the dead right after the Randy Clark conference. Check out this video: *www.markandersonministries.com/videos/lakshay-raised-from-the-dead.*

The Lord Sends Bees and Defends His Own In India

*"Moreover the LORD your **God will send the hornet** among them until those who are left, who hide themselves from you, are destroyed. You shall not be terrified of them; for the LORD your God, the great and awesome God, is among you. And the LORD your **God will drive out those nations** before you little by little..."* (Deuteronomy 7:20-22).

During the conference with Randy Clark in Chandigarh, India, a pastor from the state of Madhya Pradesh told us that a

Hindu celebration was going to be held in Mandala, Madhya Pradesh from February 11-13, 2011. This celebration is called the Kum Mela, and Hindu devotees from all over the country flock to it. In the past, millions have gathered at this celebration.

The Chief Minister of Madhya Pradesh declared that at this celebration all Christians who had converted from Hinduism would be forced to reconvert to Hinduism. If they refused to do so their daughters would be sacrificed to Hindu gods all three days. This pastor requested all the conference attendees to pray for this grave situation. In the afternoon session every one lifted their voices in intercession, as Randy Clark led us in prayer. Within 24 hours, we received a report from the pastor's son in Mandala, that as the Hindu workers were setting up for the celebration, thunderous storm clouds gathered over the grounds and it began to storm and rain heavily. Once the rain abated swarms of bees blew into the grounds and began stinging the workers. The workers were forced to abandon work and flee the grounds. The bees then proceeded to make their hives all over the grounds. This was reported in the local newspaper.

As a final outcome, the Supreme Court in India has banned this celebration. It has declared that Hindu leaders are not permitted to even enter Mandala and the Chief Minister has been ordered to maintain peace, law and order in Mandala.

Gungun (small child) - had a hole in her heart. Felt a hand touch her and felt lightness.

Preety - had pain in eyes and family problems. Lord spoke to her "all your problems are gone."

Vandana - Jesus appeared to her saying "you will be OK." She had suffered with asthma and epilepsy.

Neelam - Suffered with Jaundice (swollen liver) and was bedridden. Jesus appeared to her and caressed her while in bed telling her to go the campaign to be healed! Testifies of her healing!

Vimla - Head had not healed after a brain operation. There was a gap in her head and a bone was out of place. She felt the presence of the Lord; was completely healed. Could hit her head with no pain.

Victor - Was very sick, unable to walk, had family problems and was depressed. He believed he would be healed at the campaign. His family mocked him for wanting to go and would not take him to campaign. Jesus healed him of everything.

Rajendra Prasad - Had 3 broken bones in arm! Healed by Jesus!

Prabha - Came to the stage in tears! Was blind! Saw a bright light and her eyes were opened!

12 year old **Vineet** - Had pain in lungs! Holy Spirit touched him and Jesus said "son you are healed, go up and testify!" He immediately came and started boldly testifying what Jesus had done.

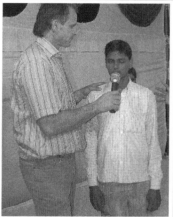

Momine - Had no circulation in right side face, could not blink his eye or speak clearly. After prayer in Jesus name, completely healed!

Many gather to hear about Jesus - In first ever citywide open air campaign in Moradabad, Uttar Pradesh, India. 11,500 turned to Christ in 5 days.

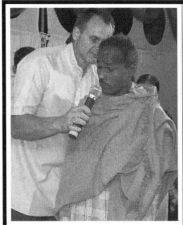

Prem Lal - Deaf and blind - 6 years! Healed by Jesus!

Santosh - Had manifested with demons starting the first night. Found freedom in Christ the last night.

On the final night our custom is to have all the participating pastors introduced so the many who came to Christ would go to their churches. During the first Sunday after the campaign each church averaged 5 to 6 new families. Now churches began following up those who filled out decision cards.

Reshab - Hears and speaks for the first time in his life after healed by Christ.

Shankar - Felt a hand pull the sickness out of his body.

Arvind Kumar - Was deaf! Now hears after Jesus opens his ears!

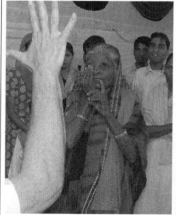

Guddi - Had a blind eye and tumor on elbow! Healed by Jesus!

Mrs. Kaddy - Suffered with cataracts, diabetes and was crippled. Healed by Jesus!

Alice - Blind and body racked with pain! Healed by Jesus!

Ganbahadur - Was paralyzed! Now dances for joy after Jesus healed him!

Kallu - Was deaf, had poor vision, and an ulcer all healed by Jesus.

Shalu had a miscarriage because her uterus was out of place. She felt an invisible hand move her uterus back into place.

Jyoti had to be carried to the meeting as she had been ill for months and could not walk. Her legs had turned blue. During mass prayer she was instantly energized by Holy Spirit and walked up and testified.

When our worship leader **Samarpan Sean** led us into an extended time of worship as everyone was worshipping, Mark asked if anyone had an encounter with Jesus or angels or was healed as result of that. Hands went up all over the crowd.

Sushma could barely speak and was shaking uncontrollably as she testified of seeing an angel whose head reached the top of the tent. She experienced severe heat and coolness after the angel touched her. She was instantly set free of the demons that were throwing her to the ground and making her cut herself the night before.

Ritika, a young girl had been praying for her mother who had stones in the kidneys and was scheduled for an operation. Ritika experienced extreme heat and began to speak in tongues and her mother felt the stones dissolve.

Mala Devi, a widow, was dying of breast cancer. She had come to Sundernagar to visit the temples, to try the appease the Hindu gods before she died. She wandered from one Hindu temple to another finding no peace. Someone invited her to the meeting. During worship she fell down. Then she felt an unseen hand lift her up. It was Jesus. She felt the oozing in her breasts stop. She said that now she has no fear of death as she knew she would be with Jesus.

We watched **Ranvir** shaking during worship. He testified that he saw a very handsome man in a white robe with longish hair on the stage smiling and waving to him. It was Jesus. Seeing Jesus waving at him, we asked Ranvir what did that make you feel like. He said he wanted to go hang out with Jesus.

Bimla - Saw Jesus in front of her wearing a crown. He placed His hand on her head and her body felt like boiling hot water & she was instantly healed of knee pain - **Sundarnagar,Himachal Pradesh, India June 7, 2013.**

Deaf and partially blind for many years. Instantly healed by Jesus during outreach on the streets of **Ullan Bator, Mongolia August 1992.**

CHAPTER 6

Why Did Jesus, God The Creator, Need To Be Born On Earth?

1 John 3:8 states, *For this purpose the Son of God was manifested, that He might **destroy the works of the devil.*** Jesus is called the second Adam. The first Adam lost so much when he gave his authority to Satan in the beginning but when Jesus defeated Satan at the cross and rose victoriously much of it was restored. After being raised from the dead, Jesus said, *"All authority has been given to Me in heaven and on earth"* (Matthew 28:18). Then He gave it to us and restored to us our inherent authority. (see Mark 16:15-18, Matthew 28:18-20).

Religious tradition and many Christians claim that Jesus performed miracles and cast out demons because He was God in the flesh, or that He was the divine Son of God, thereby exonerating themselves from the need to walk in the same power and authority He did. This is partially true. But this is how Satan operates, he puts out truth mixed with lies and slowly believers are taken off course from what the Word says. Jesus **was God** in the flesh, He **was the Son of God,** but He did not perform great miracles as a result of those reasons. That would have been contrary to His word in Genesis 1:26-28. Every person born on Earth was given authority on the Earth. That is why Jesus had to be born on this Earth to have authority. He performed these miracles because of two reasons; first, **He was born on this planet.** Second, He was **anointed by Holy Spirit** to use that authority. We have access to the same. We will touch on the second reason later.

First of all, the scripture shows us plainly that He did not operate as God in the flesh while on the earth. Phillipians 2:5-7 says, *let this mind be in you, which was also in Christ Jesus: who, being in the form of God, thought it not robbery to be **equal with God: but made Himself of no reputation** and took upon Him the form of a servant, and was **made in the likeness of men.*** Here it states He had no problem being God but **made Himself of no reputation with God.** The word **no reputation** in the Greek is the word **Kenoo.** It means to make void, of none effect, laid aside equality with or the form of God, deprive of force, render vain, useless, of no effect, cause a thing to be seen to be empty, hollow. The American Standard Bible states in verse 7 *but emptied himself, taking the form of a servant, being made in the likeness of men.* **Jesus laid aside His privileges** of being God. The New International Version says *rather, he made himself nothing by taking the very nature of a servant, being made in human likeness.* Jesus referred to Himself as the Son of man more than He referred to Himself as the Son of God. Jesus did not operate in divine power but from the position of being born here and being anointed by the Holy Spirit, through the baptism of Holy Spirit. The sons and daughters of man are the ones who have authority on this earth according to Genesis 1:26-28 and Psalms 115:16. That is one reason Jesus laid aside His privileges of being God when He came to Earth.

Genesis 1:26 says God made us in 'His image and **likeness**' (Hebrew- an exact duplicate in kind). Notice Philippians 2:7 says that Jesus, God our Creator was made in the '**likeness of men**' (an exact duplicate of man). God made us in His likeness and then came to earth to identify with mankind by becoming a man, taking on man's likeness. Philippians 2:8 says *And being found in the appearance as a man, He humbled Himself and became obedient to the point of death, even death of the cross.* Think of the price the God of creation made to become a man and pay for our salvation spirit, soul, and body. He was beaten, lied about, spit upon, punched, mocked, a crown of thorns shoved through his skull, whipped 39 times with a cat of nine tails, spikes driven through His wrists and feet and hung on a cross. All the while *He opened not His mouth; He was led as a lamb to the slaughter, And as a sheep before its shearers is silent* (Isaiah 53:7). What a price our humble God paid to become like us and redeem us!

However, Jesus needed more than just an earthly birth to use His authority over the works of the devil. He also needed the anointing of Holy Spirit. Matthew 3:16-17 shows us the turning point in Jesus' ministry where the power of God was unleashed upon Him. It says, *and Jesus, when He was baptized, went up straightway out of the water: and, lo the heavens were opened unto Him, and He saw the **Spirit of God** descending like a dove, and **lighting upon Him:** and a voice from heaven, saying, "this is my beloved Son, in whom I am well pleased."* Until the Holy Spirit descended on Jesus in Matthew 3:17, there is not one recorded miracle performed by Him. His miracle working power came after the Holy Spirit came upon Him, when He was 30 years old.

If Jesus performed miracles because He was God in the flesh or the Divine Son of God as tradition teaches us, why didn't He do miracles before Holy Spirit descended on Him in Matthew 3:16-17? Surely He was just as much God in the flesh and the Divine Son of God before this event took place. Did Jesus perform miracles as a teenager? No! Did Jesus perform miracles in His 20s? No! Why? Two main reasons! He had to operate under the authority given to a man, born on the earth. He also needed to partner with Holy Spirit in order to carry out His authority. He was not baptized in Holy Spirit until He was 30 years old. He put Himself in that place because of what He stated in the creation of mankind (see Genesis 1:26-28). He was unable to perform miracles even though He was God and was the Son of God. He laid His deity aside when He came to earth as a man, operated in the authority of a man born here, and was anointed by the Holy Spirit to perform miracles. This is the pattern He set for each one of us to follow.

It was at the Jordan River where the Spirit of the Lord came on Jesus and anointed Him to preach and do miracles. After Jesus was baptized in Holy Spirit and was in the desert fasting and praying for 40 days He returned in the power of the Spirit to Galilee (ref. Luke 4:14). This was when His miracle ministry began. Jesus stood up and said at this time: *"The Spirit of the Lord is upon Me, Because He has anointed Me To preach the gospel to the poor; He has sent Me to heal the brokenhearted, To proclaim liberty to the captives And recovery of sight to the blind, To set at liberty those who are oppressed; To proclaim the acceptable year of the Lord...Today this scripture is fulfilled in your hearing"* (Luke 4:18-20). From then on miracles and healings were a regular occurrence in Jesus' ministry.

Acts 10:38 shows us how this power came into operation in Jesus' life and ministry. It says, *how God anointed Jesus of Nazareth with the **Holy Spirit** and with **power**, who went about doing good and **healing all who were oppressed** by the devil, for God was with Him.* A study of the scriptures clearly show Jesus needed to be born on earth to have authority on the earth and then be baptized in the Holy Spirit to legally take back our authority, which had been lost to Satan and for miracles to flow through Him on a regular basis.

Look again at Hebrews 2:14, it says *Inasmuch then as the children have **partaken of flesh and blood, He Himself likewise shared** in the same, that through death He might destroy him who had the power of death, that is, the devil.* Jesus Himself had to be a partaker of flesh and blood in order to do miracles on the earth. He had to die and rise again to release the body of Christ to do greater works and redeem us from the works of the devil.

The same miracle working power Jesus operated in is available to every person born on earth who has made Jesus Lord of their lives. It is not just for Jesus and a few selected followers. 1 John 2:6 says, *He who says he abides in Him ought himself also to walk just as He walked.* And just how did Jesus walk? He walked in authority, humility, boldness, integrity, love, while casting out demons, and healing the sick and infirm. We are to do the same. Jesus gave us the Great Commission in John

20:21 (Amp). *Then Jesus said to them again, "Peace to you; as the Father has sent Me, **I also send you [as My representatives].***"

Jesus said in John 14:12 *"most assuredly, I say to you, he who believes in Me, the **works that I do he will do also, and greater works than these he will do,** because I go to My Father."* What happened when Jesus went to the Father? He sent Holy Spirit to earth so we can perform the same miracles today and even greater ones through His name, in order to fulfill the Great Commission. Notice how John 14:12 does not end with a question mark. It ends with a period. Many believers can't comprehend how we could do greater works than Jesus, and question this statement made by Jesus. They say "how can we do greater miracles than Jesus?" There are more miracles happening on earth now than any other previous time in history. Even more than when Jesus walked this earth in the flesh! Stop questioning the power of Holy Spirit and start tapping into His power. Some think it is arrogance to think we can do greater works than Jesus. It is arrogance and pride to question His word and put limits on Him. Stop questioning His Word and start acting on it with authority and faith believing.

When believers start understanding their God-given authority, who they are in Christ, and start partnering with Holy Spirit, we will see more miracles, healings, signs and wonders than any other time in history. What an exciting time to be alive serving Jesus!

Our Authority In Three Realms

Jesus gave us the use of His name after ascending from Hell. We read in Mark 16:17-18 *And these signs will follow those who believe:* **In My name** *they will cast out demons; they will speak with new tongues; they will take up serpents; and if they drink anything deadly, it will by no means hurt them; they will lay hands on the sick, and they will recover."* Through His name we have authority in three realms. Look at what Philippians 2:9-11 says about Jesus and His name. *"Therefore God has highly exalted Him and given Him the name which is above every name, that at the name of Jesus* **every knee should bow,** *of those* **in heaven,** *and of those on* **earth,** *and of those* **under the earth,** *and that every tongue should confess that Jesus is Lord, to the glory of God the Father."* The name of Jesus is higher than demons of cancer, blindness, deafness, paralysis, or any other sickness or bondage. We have the use of the name of Jesus and the power of the Holy Spirit to carry out our God-given authority. Through His name we have authority in heaven, earth and in hell.

Jesus was one who walked in authority. When praying for the sick or demonized, many do not comprehend how to use their authority and the name of Jesus. Many people, while ministering to the sick, have turned it into a prayer meeting thinking praying louder or longer will cause God to answer them. Some who pray are very insecure or lack confidence and because of this see no real results. When it comes to healing, some pray: "Lord if it be your will." They sound religious but that is not how you operate in authority and faith, when it comes to healing the sick or casting out demons.

And the **prayer of faith will save the sick,** and the Lord will raise him up. And if he has committed sins, he will be forgiven (James 5:15). It is the prayer of faith, not the prayer of uncertainty that makes the difference! All we need to do is look at how Jesus prayed for the sick and demonized. He did not lay hands and pray over someone until he wore every hair off the top of their head. He never prayed for healing with the phrase 'if it be your will.' Jesus did not yell or scream to cast out demons until His voice went hoarse. He spoke to the sickness and/or demon with authority, commanding it to leave. Sickness and/ or demons obeyed His command! Why not follow his lead and pray with authority like He did? We can do the same, since we have the same Holy Spirit and the use of the name that is above all names, the name of Jesus.

Notice how Jesus, most of the time, spoke the end results and what He spoke came to pass. At times Jesus touched people or people touched Him without saying a word, virtue flowed out of Him and they were instantly healed. Once my wife

Sharmila, a tough woman who loves weightlifting, slipped on ice and fell while she was walking our dog in the hills behind our home. She was in a lot of pain. At times it brought her to tears. We prayed at times when the pain was intense and she would get some temporary relief but the injury still caused a lot of pain. A short time later we were in Redding, California to get ordained and licensed by Randy Clark and Bill Johnson. Randy introduced both of us to Bill and he shook our hands. When he shook Sharmila's hand something happened. As soon as he left she said *"My back is on fire."* I felt her back and sure enough it was on fire and soaked in sweat (in January). Later that afternoon we were listening to Randy Clark teaching at the conference when Sharmila said, *"by the way, my back does not hurt anymore."* She was completely healed just by a simple anointed handshake! This is a good example of walking in authority without even saying a word or speaking it. Just understanding authority can set you up for divine appointments like this.

Once, while teaching pastors and leaders in Mount Haugen, Papua New Guinea on the Baptism of Holy Spirit and authority, I demonstrated how to use our authority by praying over those ministers who needed healing. One minister, Nagalu Gangabu, was completely deaf in his right ear since 1976. As a demonstration of how to use our authority, I laid hands on him and commanded the deaf spirit to leave in the name of Jesus and his ear to open. He heard instantly! Many others were healed as well. This inspired the ministers that they could do the same. Then I taught them on the Baptism of Holy Spirit. Many of these ministers had never heard of this before. Many were baptized in the Holy Spirit for the first time in their life. Later I asked the ministers to put into practice what was taught. We saw tremendous results at that conference.

One powerful testimony I recalled hearing was about two of these ministers who had just learned the principles and were baptized in Holy Spirit. They made their way home through the jungle and got lost. They met an old man and asked for directions. Turns out the man was born deaf and mute. Acting upon their faith and authority, they rebuked the deaf and mute spirit, taking authority over it in Jesus' name and the man heard and spoke instantly. Then they had to do some explaining at the local village of what Jesus had done to the old man! Those ministers are just two of many ministers who have seen results as they put into practice these principles. You too can have signs and wonders following as you act upon the Word and use the authority God has instilled within us who are born on planet earth and have come into partnership with the Holy Spirit through faith in Jesus.

Dual Meaning Of The Word Power

There are two Greek words used in the New Testament for **power**. The first Greek word for power is **EXOUSIA**, which means authority, privilege, right, liberty, jurisdiction and strength. The other word is **DUNAMIS**, which means mighty work, strength, miracle, power residing in a thing by virtue of its nature and power for performing miracles. **Dunamis** is also the root of the word dynamite. By understanding these words we can see the power God gave us in Genesis 1:26-28. We can also understand why we need the Holy Spirit to carry out that authority. Let's look at these words in different passages.

Exousia is used by Jesus in Luke 10:19 He says *"Behold, I give you the authority (**exousia**) to trample on serpents and scorpions, and over all the power (**dunamis**) of the enemy, and nothing shall by any means hurt you."* The word authority here is **EXOUSIA**, the authority we were given in Genesis 1:26-28.

A good example of this kind of authority and power would be of a police officer directing traffic at a busy intersection. That police officer is given the power or authority to direct traffic. Let's say a driver does not want to stop his truck when the officer signals him to do so. Could that officer physically stop this truck? Of course not! The truck would flatten him if he tried to do that. He would have to move out of its way. The officer you could say has the authority (exousia), but not the might or power to enforce physically (dunamis). That is where the power of the law comes in and **the laws** of that land **are enforced!** The trucker is arrested and made to pay the penalty for his crime.

Within ourselves we cannot carry out our authority. Just like the officer in the example has authority to direct traffic but does not have the physical might or power to stop the truck, we have the authority but need the might and power (dunamis) of Holy Spirit to enforce our authority. Jesus said in Acts 1:8 *"But you shall receive power* (**dunamis**) *when the Holy Spirit has come upon you; and you shall be witnesses* (Greek- **someone who verifies his testimony with an exhibition of evidence, something evidential, with proof, vouch for, prove, guarantee, bears witness by death and martyr**) *to Me in Jerusalem, and in all Judea, and Samaria, and to the end of the earth."* Here the word for power is different. It literally means **miraculous ability.** When we are in partnership with the Holy Spirit, He gives us the ability to carry out our God-given authority through His **mighty power.** He is the miracle worker.

The Baptism of the Holy Spirit is something that comes after salvation. Jesus is the one who baptizes us in the Holy Spirit when we hunger for the power of the Holy Spirit to be His witness. John the Baptist said this about Jesus: *"I indeed baptize you with water unto repentance, but He who is coming after me is mightier than I, whose sandals I am not worthy to carry.*

He will baptize you with the Holy Spirit and fire" (Matthew 3:11). Just like the heavens were opened and Jesus was baptized in the Holy Spirit at the Jordan River in Matthew 3:16-17 to begin performing miracles and to carry out His authority, we need the same heavenly experience and power (dunamis) too if we want to see miracles and healings on a regular basis.

Jesus said *Blessed are those who hunger and thirst for righteousness, For they shall be filled* (Matthew 5:6). If you want to see the authority you have been given by God released in your life there needs to be a hunger to be filled, immersed, and baptized in Holy Spirit by Jesus. Whatever you hunger for you will be filled with that. You should hunger for the power of Holy Spirit in your life! If you have not experienced this yet, press in for this heavenly experience. You won't be disappointed (see Luke 11:9-13). In the book of Acts, three out of the four times it mentions being filled with the Holy Spirit it is accompanied by speaking in tongues. Being able to pray in tongues has helped release my faith and authority to perform miracles and healings in Jesus' name. Jude verse 20 says *But you, beloved, **building yourselves up** on your most holy faith, **praying in the Holy Spirit.*** Praying in tongues is praying in the Holy Spirit.

Many Muslims come forward in **Malerkotla, Punjab, India** to receive healing prayer in Jesus' name- Approximately **16,500 people came to Christ** in this four day outreach as Holy Spirit confirmed the Word of God with signs following- **October 4-9, 2004.**

Satpal Singh - Was not able to walk or stand. Had brain cancer. Completely healed by Jesus - **Sitarganj, India Oct 9, 2015.**

Bijoy Das was born blind. After praying in Jesus' name, Holy Spirit opened his blind eyes. Demonstrates he can see clearly by catching a stone and counting fingers. His miracle triggered a mighty move of God in his village and approximately 1,200 turned to Christ **- Dumdumi, West Bengal, India Spring 2002.**

CHAPTER 7

Spiritual Warfare And Our Authority

In the early 1980s I was working as a carpenter in Aspen, Colorado on a large townhouse building. I was looking for opportunities to share Christ with my co-workers but had little success. Finally one day at lunch one of the workers asked if I wanted to go get high on marijuana and get drunk with the rest of the crew after work. I told him I did not need that because Jesus gives me a great high. He told me "don't tell me about your Jesus." Little did he know the Bible calls our God '**The Most High**.' I would rather get high on 'The Most High' than some substitute or counterfeit.

Even though this guy did not want to hear anything about Jesus he started going around the job site telling everyone about the Jesus fanatic at work. With his help I ended up taking five guys to church one night for a midweek service. Three of them spoke Spanish and did not understand the preaching but the other two were Americans. The American men really enjoyed the service. I asked one man, Noah if he wanted to accept Christ that night. He told me "not now" but that he was interested in going to the church again. I told him I could take him on Sunday.

Later that week we worked together and were scheduled for overtime on Saturday but he never showed up to work. That night at about 3:30am Holy Spirit woke me up. I waited on Him to find out what was happening. He transmitted to my spirit man, 'bind the spirit of suicide and spirit of death.' I took authority and bound those spirits and then prayed in tongues, allowing Holy Spirit to pray through me. Finally after praying for a while I had peace and went back to sleep.

The next morning I went to pick up Noah for church service. He stayed in a place where many of the workers from out of town stayed. I went in and nobody was around. So I began leaving. As I passed by a bedroom door I heard a faint sound from inside the room and felt like I needed to open it. I was not prepared for what I saw. Blood was all over the room. An empty bottle of sleeping pills was on the dresser. When the pills had not worked, Noah cut his wrist. When cutting his wrist did not work, he cut his main artery and blood was all over the room. He was laying in a puddle of his own blood. The only thing that had kept him from bleeding to death was that his arm was folded and blood had begun to dry.

I called for the ambulance and called the church to pray. Noah was put in intensive care. I asked my Pastor, Bruce Porter, to visit him the next day because I had to be at work. Pastor Bruce went to the hospital and found Noah awake and recovering. He found out that everything that could go wrong for Noah had gone wrong. Noah's wife left him. Someone stole his luggage and nothing good was happening. He decided to take his life. When Pastor Bruce shared the good news of Jesus with Noah, he received Christ as his Lord. Like a lightbulb, something turned on on the inside. All of a sudden he had a reason to live. We ended up traveling to Minnesota together, and I counseled him a bit in his walk with Christ before we parted ways.

I thank Holy Spirit for leading me to share Christ at work even though the response was not good at first. I thank Him for transmitting to my spirit man to bind the spirits of suicide and death, take authority over those demons in Jesus' name and pray in the tongues for Noah. If I had not been obedient to my partner, Holy Spirit, Noah would be in hell today without Christ. We need Holy Spirit to transmit to our spirit man things that pertain to the present and the future. We need to pray in tongues and use our God-given authority.

Demonic Warfare And Our Authority

Daniel was in a season of mourning, fasting and prayer. As he persevered in prayer, the angel Gabriel appeared to him and revealed some things that were occurring behind the scene in the spiritual realm, and why it was taking so long for his prayers to be answered. *Suddenly, a hand touched me, which made me tremble on my knees and on the palms of my hands. And he said to me, "O Daniel, man greatly beloved, understand the words that I speak to you, and stand upright, for I have now been sent to you." While he was speaking this word to me, I stood trembling. Then he said to me, "Do not fear, Daniel, for from the first day that you set your heart to understand, and to humble yourself before your God, **your words were heard;** and I have come because of your words. **But the prince of the kingdom of Persia withstood me** twenty-one days; and behold, **Michael, one of the chief princes, came to help me,** for I had been left alone there with the kings of Persia. Now I have come to make you understand what will happen to your people in the latter days, for the vision refers to many days yet to come"* (Daniel 10:10-14).

This passage gives us insight into struggles that are taking place over nations and reveals that we can't be passive, but need to rise up with authority and persevere in prayer for nations and governments. The prince of the kingdom of Persia was a demonic spirit (fallen angel). It delayed Gabriel from breaking through with the answer to Daniel's crucial prayers. Daniel was unaware of this struggle and continued pressing in to get the answer. As Daniel waited for the answer, Gabriel and another angel Micheal were contending with the prince of the kingdom of Persia.

Ephesians 6:12 (Amp) spells out clearly. *For our struggle is not against flesh and blood [contending only with physical opponents], but against the rulers, against the powers, against the world forces of this [present] darkness, against the spiritual forces of wickedness in the heavenly (supernatural) places.* It so important to understand our God-given authority, who we are in Christ and to know *the weapons of our warfare are not carnal but mighty in God for pulling down strongholds* (2 Corinthians 10:4). There is a demonic plan and agenda for our nation just as there is a Godly plan and agenda for our nation. Our focus always has to be Christ centered but at the same time we can't ignore evil trying to take control of places of influence, especially government. We can't remain passive to demonic plans for our nation. We have seen in the USA what a passive attitude towards evil trying to set it self up in our nation does when we do nothing. It causes our nation to go downhill quickly. Thank God the Body of Christ has risen up in authority in the USA in recent years, to contend and stand against evil trying to set itself up over our nation. *To keep Satan from taking advantage of us; for we are not ignorant of his schemes* (2 Corinthians 2:11 Amp).

We have things so much better than Daniel had it. We live under a new covenant since Christ went to the cross. We have access to the name of Jesus and the power of Holy Spirit to go with our authority. Jesus defeated Satan and his demons and rose victorious. Now all we are really doing is enforcing his victory over hell. *When He had disarmed the rulers and authorities [those supernatural forces of evil operating against us], He **made a public example of them** [exhibiting them as captives in His triumphal procession], having **triumphed over them through the cross*** (Colossians 2:15 Amp). Any warfare we do now needs to come from our position of victory in Christ.

Sharmila and I are very involved in USA politics and stay informed. I wrote a book to bring awareness on issues and the candidates during the last national election, entitled **The Damaging Effect of the Religious Spirit in Politics.** Why are we involved and informed? Because we believe that what happens in the United States government, in Washington, DC, greatly impacts the entire world. We are not easily given to conspiracy theories, but seek the truth and root of the problems that face our nation.

Paul words it well in Ephesians 2:2 (Amp). *You were* ***following the ways of this world*** *[influenced by this present age],* ***in accordance with the prince of the power of the air (Satan),*** *the spirit who is now at work in the disobedient [the* ***unbelieving,*** ***who fight against the purposes of God].*** Many who don't know Christ are puppets for demonic spirits. These spirits seek to influence our culture and its mindset. We can see this all over the world. With that knowledge, knowing who we are in Christ and using the authority we have though the name of Jesus we intercede for our nation and other nations. What we find so cool about our great God is when you follow His prompting to pray for certain issues He answers. Sharmila and I pray daily for our president and his administration. So many times we have prayed over certain issues of concerns over our nation. Then we watch the answer to that prayer on the evening news. Keep in mind you will not hear about answers to prayer in most of our media outlets. We also pray a lot for our very bias media and their agendas.

We need to stand in the gap and intercede for our nation, lest it be overrun by evil (See Ezekiel 22:30). We can't just be passive but need to be actively interceding with our God-given authority for those in power. *First of all, then, I urge that petitions (specific requests), prayers, intercessions (prayers for others) and thanksgivings be offered on behalf of all people, for kings and all* *who are in [positions of] high authority, **so that we may live a peaceful and quiet life** in all godliness and dignity. This [kind of praying] is good and acceptable and pleasing in the sight of God our Savior, who **wishes all people to be saved** and to come to the knowledge and recognition of the [divine] truth* (1 Timothy 2:1-4 Amp). Interceding for those in authority can also lead to the salvation of the lost in our nations according to verse 4.

I am very grateful that as a young man called into ministry in the late 1970's I had the opportunity to travel with and learn a lot about healing and deliverance ministry from an old time Gospel Tent Preacher by the name of Dick Hendren. He and his wife Tonna headed up **He Cares For You Ministries** together, until Dick passed away last year. Dick had a powerful healing and deliverance ministry. For the first time in my life I was exposed to the demonic realm and how through Jesus we have victory over demons. So much of what I learned during those days about casting out demons and intercession I have taken all around the world literally seeing thousands set free from demonic torment and pain. It has also helped me when interceding for those in authority. I will always be grateful for my time spent with those two. I have a lot of good memories working with the Hendrens, seeing for the first time in my life the authority we have in Christ and the supernatural power of Holy Spirit.

Proof For Atheists

Jesus said *But you will receive **power and ability when the Holy Spirit comes upon you;** and you will be **My witnesses** [to tell people about Me] both in Jerusalem and in all Judea, and Samaria, and even to the ends of the earth* (Acts 1:8 Amp). The Greek word for **witnesses** refers to someone who has the ability to **back their testimony** of Jesus Christ with **miracles or proof** just like the early church did in the book of Acts. The word *witness* is used time and time again in the book of Acts and it referred to someone who had the power of Holy Spirit to **demonstrate by miracles the resurrection of Jesus Christ.**

Another word for witness in Greek is bears witness by death or martyr. Our early church forefathers were truly witnesses for Christ in every way. Ten of the eleven remaining disciples of Jesus died a martyr's death after Jesus resurrection. Many today would think they died for a lie. Think about it! Why would anyone lay their life down for a lie, especially a lie they came up with? The disciples are the ones who saw Jesus after He was raised from the dead and spread the news about His resurrection. They had been convinced that Jesus was Lord and God by His resurrection, His teachings, and what they saw Him do as they followed Him.

They were also convinced by seeing His undeniable

miracles happening after He was raised from the dead and they were filled with Holy Spirit. After Jesus was raised from the dead He told them *these signs will follow those who believe: In My name they will cast out demons; they will speak with new tongues; they will take up serpents; and if they drink anything deadly, it will by no means hurt them; they will lay hands on the sick, and they will recover* (Mark 16:17-18). What better way to prove Christ is alive than to reproduce the same miracles and healings that He did. This is something Jesus said after He was raised from the dead, as proof He is alive today. These disciples of Jesus demonstrated the resurrection power of God with miracles, healings, signs, wonders and when it came down to it they freely laid their lives down as martyrs (witnesses) for Him because they knew it was true.

The religious leaders of Jesus day opposed Him and did not believe in Him. When they were arguing with Him He said this: *If I do not do the works of My Father [that is, the **miracles that only God could perform**], then do not believe Me. But if I am doing them, even if you do not believe Me or have faith in Me, [at least] believe the works [that I do—admit that they are the works of God], so that you may know and keep on knowing [clearly— without any doubt] that the Father is in Me, and I am in the Father [that is, I am One with Him]* (John 10:37-38 Amp). How do you prove Jesus is who He claims to be? How do you know the Bible is true compared to all the other religions' holy books? Let a miracle settle the issue that Jesus is alive and who He claims to be.

Ted Turner

2 Timothy 3:5 talks about the last days we live in. It says *holding to a form of [**outward**] **godliness (religion)**, although they have **denied its power** [for their conduct nullifies their claim of faith]. **Avoid such people** and keep far away from them.* Many Christians have embraced the belief that God does both good and bad because of the influence of Greek Philosophy mixed with Western Christianity. It has created a powerless form of Christianity that Paul tells us to avoid. They believe God causes suffering, sickness and disease and do not pray in authority, compassion and faith to help the suffering. How many people have looked in on Christianity and seen this type of powerless Christianity and have become atheists, God haters, agnostics, etc?

The famous billionaire Ted Turner, an atheist for most of his life, has spewed hatred for God and Christianity. It seems odd that an atheist, someone who does not believe in God, can hate someone he does not believe exists. *The fool has said in his heart, "There is no God." They are corrupt, They have done abominable works, There is none who does good* (Psalms 14:1). Ted, now 79, in recent years has softened his stance on Christianity a bit. He claims to be more agnostic now. As a businessman, he is the founder of the world famous CNN News Network. In 1990, Turner made a speech to the American Humanist Association (Atheists). During that tirade he made his (in)famous quip: *"Christianity is a religion for losers."*[1]

He has made a lot of other remarks that showed he despised Christianity and God for most of this life. On March 7, 2001 in CNN's Washington, DC newsroom Ted Turner addressed the staff on the occasion of CNN anchor Bernard Shaw's retirement party and it happened to fall on Ash Wednesday. Many of the CNN staffers had visited church that morning, and some still had an ash cross on their foreheads. Before Mr. Turner began his remarks, he noticed the ash and quipped, *"What are you, a bunch of Jesus freaks? You ought to be working for Fox."* [2] Fox is a news network that expresses conservative and Christian views, that would rarely be found on Ted Turner's news network, CNN.

What made him so hostile to Christianity? When Ted was a young boy he wanted to be a missionary. He watched his sister Mary Jean suffer with Lupus for five years and die a horrible and painful death. Ted's father said *"If that's the type of God he is, I want nothing to do with him"* and then shot himself after seeing Mary Jean pass away. Shortly after that Ted totally abandoned his faith in God and became an atheist, but not just an atheist, a very hostile voice against God and Christianity. Ted recalled, *"It just seemed so unfair because she (Mary Jean) hadn't done anything wrong. What had she done wrong? And I could not get any answers. Christianity couldn't give me any answers to that. So my faith was shaken somewhat."* Since that time he has spent almost his entire life hating anything about Christianity.[3]

How many others are out there raised in Christians circles, but turned off to a lifeless powerless form of Christianity? We need to rise up with the authority we have been given by God, partner with Holy Spirit and be the witnesses He has called us to be in order to show this world Jesus is alive and is truly Lord, Healer and Deliverer. We need to show people He is not the author of evil, as Ted Turner believes. He is not in a bad mood and angry all the time with humanity. In fact He is in a good mood because He is a good God. He is not the author of bad or evil things that happen in life like natural disasters, sickness or disease. If we do not rise up and use our God-given authority many more like Ted Turner will fall away from our loving, compassionate Christ and oppose the Gospel, like Ted has done most of his life because of a very distorted view of God and poor theology.

The First Demon Cast Out By Jesus

Lets take a look at the first demon Jesus cast out to learn something about authority. *"Then they went to Capernaum, and immediately on the Sabbath He entered the synagogue and taught. And they were astonished at His teaching, for He **taught** them as one **having authority** (exousia), and not as the scribes. Now there was a man in their synagogue with an unclean spirit. And he cried out, saying 'let us alone! What have we to do with You, Jesus of Nazareth? Did you come to destroy us? I know who you are- **the Holy One of God!'** But Jesus rebuked him, saying, 'Be quiet, and come out of him!' And when the unclean spirit had convulsed him and cried out with a loud voice, he came out of him. Then they were all amazed, so that they questioned among themselves, saying, 'What is this? What new doctrine (teaching) is this? For **with authority (exousia) He commands even the unclean spirits, and they obey Him.'** And immediately His fame spread throughout all the region around Galilee"* (Mark 1:21-28).

Jesus taught and cast out demons with authority (exousia) and confidence. The people were amazed at the authority in which Jesus operated. Some are of the opinion that to minister with confidence and authority is prideful. Jesus was the perfect example of someone who walked in **Humility**. For more on this check out my book *Humility the Hidden Key to Walking in Signs and Wonders.* Humility also **gave Jesus the confidence** to operate in authority. There is no insecurity or lack of confidence when we operate in true biblical humility. We will cover more on how authority, humility and submission work hand in hand in the next chapter.

I also want to bring your attention to something very strange. Notice what the unclean spirit said to Jesus. *"Did you come to destroy us?* **I know who you are- the Holy One of God."** Think about it! Why would a demon let everyone know that Jesus was the Holy One of God? Demons are not ones to glorify Jesus, God the Son. There had to be a reason for this demon to say this. This demon thought he had the legal right to stay in this man and Jesus legally could not do anything about it because He was God. Remember Jesus stripped Himself of his deity when He came to earth operating as the son of a man (ref. Phil. 2:6-8). He was born on earth, had authority by being born on earth and He had been baptized in the Holy Spirit. This demon did not take these things into account.

Personally I believe this demon said that, because he knew God, Jesus, the Creator had given authority to mankind to rule and reign on this earth and mankind had given his authority over to Satan who had become the god or ruler of this world, as it states in 2 Corinthians 4:3-4. He knew God could not operate or go contrary to His Word in Genesis 1:26-28. Man was given the authority on earth, not God. God had to operate through a man to use his authority or power. It was the same for Satan.

Adam gave his authority to Satan by submitting to his lies. In order for mankind to carry out their authority and to operate in miracles or healings on the earth they need the help of the Holy Spirit. It is quite similar for evil men and women to bring about evil in this world. Many work in partnership with evil spirits to do evil things. Each person has his or her own free will. Who they yield to is their choice, whether to God to do good or demons to do evil. For the most part, for God or evil spirits to have authority on the earth, they work through those who are born on this planet and will willingly submit to them to do their bidding. Jesus, God in the flesh was born on this earth. He could legally operate in the authority He gave man in the beginning of time. This totally caught this demon and hell off guard.

Through God's Word we can see that we are to be dependent on the Holy Spirit to carry out our authority. We also realize that God needs men and women yielded to the Holy Spirit to carry out His plan on the earth. We need to be in partnership with Holy Spirit to carry out God's plan on the earth.

Every person born on earth has authority, including Jesus, who was born in the flesh. Once again 1 John 4:3 says *and every spirit that does not confess that Jesus* **Christ (Greek -the anointed one)** *has come in the flesh is not of God. And this is the spirit of Anti-Christ which you heard was coming and already is in the world."*

Jesus, the Christ, the anointed one, came in the flesh, stripped Himself of His deity and came as the Son of man enabling him to use the **authority (exousia)** God gave man in the beginning of time along with the **power (dunamis)** of the Holy Spirit to destroy the works of the devil.

It is God's desire for His people to understand the authority He has given us, in order to lay an unshakable foundation out of which miracles will flow. When the Body of Christ comes into this understanding, miracles and healings will become a regular occurrence. Then towns, states, and countries will experience a great influx of souls coming to Christ. Therefore let us arise and take hold of the authority we were destined to walk in, since Christ defeated Satan and restored our authority.

Isaac Mosher a 9th grader who was born with Goldhar Syndrome (deformities) was healed by Jesus and was able to hold his head up for the first time in his life - **Detroit Lakes, MN October 5, 2008.**

Shasibala - 63 years old. Completely lost her memory and speech from Alzheimers disease. Healed by Christ. Regained memory and speech - **Ambala, Harayana, India October 31, 2012.**

CHAPTER 8

The Centurion's Faith

*A certain centurion's servant, who was dear to him, was sick and ready to die. So when he heard about Jesus, he sent elders of the Jews to Him, pleading with Him to come and heal his servant. And when they came to Jesus, they begged Him earnestly, saying that the one for whom He should do this was deserving, "for he loves our nation, and has built us a synagogue." Then Jesus went with them. And when he was already not far from the house, the centurion sent friends to Him, saying to Him, "Lord do not trouble yourself, for **I am not worthy** that You should enter my roof. Therefore I did not even think myself worthy to come to You. But **say the word,** and my servant **will be healed.** For I also am a man placed under authority, having soldiers under me. And I say to one, 'Go,' and he goes; and to another, 'Come,' and he comes; and to my servant, 'Do this,' and* *he does it." When Jesus heard these things, He marveled at him, and turned around and said to the crowd that followed Him, "I say to you, I have not found* **such great faith, not even in Israel.**" *And those who were sent, returning to the house, found the servant well who had been sick* (Luke 7:2-10).

In verse 9 Jesus says, *"I have not found such* **great faith,** *not even in Israel."* What was so great about the centurion's faith? This man understood the importance of authority and humility. Here is a centurion in the Roman army humbling himself to receive from Jesus. Many in a high position would never think of humbling themselves to receive something from someone they considered to be inferior. He understood that, in and of himself, he was not worthy that Jesus should do anything for him. Some have ignored this key ingredient of humility and have come across with an arrogant attitude. The centurion said he was unworthy because he realized that His beliefs were not in line with God's way of doing things, and thus, he was not worthy that Jesus should come to his house. His humility, understanding of authority, and faith led Jesus to declare that he had the greatest faith He had seen. Jesus has made us worthy of nothing less than His ultimate best. However in and of ourselves, we are not worthy. We need to keep in mind that it is only because of what He did at Calvary.

God **resists** [Greek: ranges in battle against] *the proud but* *gives **grace to the humble*** (James 4:6; 1 Peter 5:5). If there is anything I have learned from all my years in ministry, it is that every blessing or gift from God comes only by His grace. Who gets the grace? The humble of heart! This centurion was very humble, especially for someone who was a high ranking officer. Many think that to receive a healing or miracle they have to do certain things; then somehow they might receive a miracle or healing from Jesus. Jesus healed many different ways. The focus needs to be on Jesus and on the fact that everything good only comes by His grace alone. We cannot work up grace. **Humility helps us be a candidate for His grace.**

Other concepts the centurion understood are found in verse 7. He knew Jesus had the authority to speak the word and heal his servant, and he asked Him to do so. If we want to see success in a healing ministry, people need to know that we have the authority in Jesus' name to minister to them, and then they need to allow us to do so. We cannot force healing on people. Generally people need to pursue Jesus' healing power and want prayer. They need to put a draw on Jesus' healing power.

Notice once again the power of words. This man believed in the power of Jesus' spoken word. The majority of people receive healing in our campaigns when we take authority, using the name of Jesus over sickness or infirmities without even laying hands on them. As mentioned earlier, as Christians, our words have authority and produce life if our words are positive.

Let me take a little detour here. Does everybody get healed in our meetings or when we pray one on one? I wish they did! Some will come back another night and get healed. Some may never be healed. Does that mean God does not want them healed? Not at all! There are *road blocks to healing*. Check out my book **Overcoming Roadblocks to Healing.** Holy Spirit has healed many in spite of hindrances. For some though it is just a matter of getting around the road block to healing or deliverance in their life to find victory.

I can't explain why all do not get healed but I know what God's Word tells me concerning healing. I can choose to live my life by the negative experiences and build my doctrine and belief system on those negative experiences or choose to base my life on what the Word says. We should not live our lives by the exceptions to God's Word. We have been given authority in this life to heal and deliver people through the power of Jesus' name. For the many that have not been healed when we have prayed, there are thousands who have been healed and delivered. If you do not step out in faith and authority to bring healing and deliverance to others you will never experience His power available to you. I can't explain all the exceptions to the Word of God, nor can most people. But I will always trust His Word with unwavering faith even in the midst of negative experiences! That is the kind of attitude the Centurion had. When our faith gets to that level that is when we begin to see results that move mountains.

Interceding With Authority For The Critically Ill

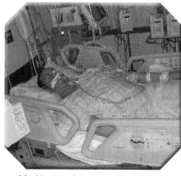

Mark's son **Jesse** on life support. Doctors did not know if he would live or die- Burlington, Vermont January 2003.

One year later, **Jesse** preaching at Bible school completely leukemia free! Leukemia free to this day! Jesse was instantly healed of leukemia. His full story is in chapter 8 of Mark's book **Overcoming Roadblocks to Healing. Published by Global Awakening.**

Mark's parents **John & Jane Anderson** enjoying their retirement, many years after Jane was miraculously healed of breast cancer. The doctor said a mystery had taken place in her blood cells and she no longer had cancer. Never to have cancer again!

Over the years Sharmila and I have interceded for a lot of

people who have had cancer. A number of them, some friends, have passed away. We could not and still can't understand why they passed away. At the same time we keep running into people who have had cancer years ago that we interceded for (some very close to death) and they are alive and well today. Some share how the prayers of the saints prevailed and they are alive today because of those prayers. So what do you do? Should we give up praying with authority for those ill with cancer because of negative experiences, or do we keep praying and believing for miracles for those who are suffering with cancer or other serious sickness and need our prayers? Sharmila and I choose to encourage ourselves with the testimonies of those that recovered and are doing well today, and believe for more to be healed as we intercede.

I have also seen first hand the power of intercession in Jesus name for both my mother and son Jesse who were healed of cancer when the odds were against them (Jesse had leukemia). They are alive and well today and never had cancer again after they were supernaturally healed by Christ.

The following testimony is of mighty woman of God whom I have known for many years. Hazel and her husband George Hill are founders of the Victory Churches International, a church planting movement that is all over the world *www. victoryint.org.* Hazel started feeling ill in August of 1990 and thought it was because of her much overseas travel. The conditions got worse. Later on she was diagnosed with cancer and also suffered a blood clot on her lungs. She became deathly ill. Many hundreds, if not thousands of people interceded for this woman of God who was fighting for her life. I remember hearing about her illness and the dire situation and began praying for her. I remember once late at night Holy Spirit came on

Hazel Hill, alive and well today, sharing the Gospel of Jesus Christ around the world, after being healed of cancer and a blood clot.

me with a strong spirit of intercession for Hazel while living in the countryside of Western New York State. I could not ignore it and I prayed it through. I believe during this time many people were interceding for Hazel. They did not give up!

Things in the natural looked bleak for Hazel. But suddenly one day things took a change for the better. Here is the story from her close friend Debbie Williams who stayed in the hospital room with her during those days. This is from Hazel's book *Adventure, Romance, and Revival www.victoryint.org. "Our days began with prayer, worship, and confession of God's Word. Washings and a biopsy had been taken during the operation* and were being analyzed. We focused on the only One who could help—His name is Jesus! We waited. One night after retiring, I remember hearing angels in the atmosphere. In fact we both heard them at the same time. Out of the darkness of our room Hazel said, "Did you hear that? There must be a chapel next door." I told her that the chapel was eight floors below us. **We were silent as we listened to a multitude of people praying, speaking in tongues, doing warfare. As we listened, faintly at first were the words, "We have the Victory, We have the Victory!" The voices seemed to roll up the wall to our right making an arc, building to a crescendo then rolling down the opposite wall and tapped off to silence. The presence of God was real and tangible in that room. We had a visitation of God!** We slept.

The next morning Hazel woke, sat up in bed and prophesied that this day would be a day of new beginnings. First the doctor came in with good news, "The washings are clear." Then another doctor, "The biopsy is also clear." The nurse who was monitoring the blood clot arrived. She proclaimed, "There is no more blood clot here! Praise the Lord! We really did have the victory and it really was a New Day!

The operation was a success and all the cancer was removed. The doctor suggested a series of eight chemo sessions for Hazel after this to make sure nothing was left behind. Hazel and George prayed about it and decided to do it. From that day onward at the hospital she never had cancer again, is healthy and still travels all over the world proclaiming the goodness of Jesus to this day.

In 1994 George and Hazel were instrumental in getting Sharmila (who lived in India) and I together. Sharmila and I hit it off a short time later while meeting in India. We were married on May 20, 1995 in New Delhi. I am grateful to George and Hazel for helping make that happen. I am so glad Holy Spirit came on me and many others to intercede, take authority over cancer and death in Jesus' name when Hazel was fighting for her life. Never give up on your loved ones. *Jesus Christ is the same yesterday, today, and forever* (Hebrews 13:8). Just like the prayers of the saints prevailed in Hazel's life they can also prevail in many other lives as well. Miracles are taking place in abundance today as people use their authority in Christ to intercede for the suffering and ill.

The centurion also understood that another important facet of faith and humility was to be under authority (see Luke 7:8). This is the same thing that is mentioned in 1 Peter 5:5 (Amp), *Likewise, you younger men [of lesser rank and experience], be subject to your elders [seek their counsel]; and all of you, clothe yourselves with humility toward one another [tie on the servant's apron], for God is opposed to the proud [the disdainful, the presumptuous, and He defeats them], but He gives grace to the humble.* Some never operate in healing and miracles because they are too proud to submit or to learn from somebody who is proven in that area of ministry. To walk in true authority and faith, we should be accountable and in submission to others.

Much of what I am doing today I learned from other men of God who were successful in healing ministry. It helps when we learn from those who have "been there and done that." We believe there is a place of great blessing and a place of protection when we are under authority and accountable to others, to be held to a certain standard. Having no connection to submission, being critical, prideful, and unteachable can keep us from tapping into Christ's healing power. Healings and miracles become very inconsistent in an environment like that.

*And let us consider [thoughtfully] how we may encourage one another to love and to do good deeds, **not forsaking our meeting together [as believers for worship and instruction]**, as is the habit of some, but encouraging one another; and all the more [faithfully] as you see the day [of Christ's return] approaching* (Hebrews 10:24-25 Amp). We are admonished to come together for worship and instruction. One reason is: *As **iron sharpens iron,** So one man sharpens [and influences] another [through discussion]* (Proverbs 27:17 Amp). In fellowship, one person who has gone through circumstances and gained the victory can share with another how they can avoid the pitfalls and overcome. It makes it that much easier for the other person to excel. Also there is power in united corporate action to get things done for the Kingdom of God. In that kind of atmosphere when the Body of Christ understands authority miracles and healing flow easily. When we are scattered, doing our own little things, miracles and healings become inconsistent.

Sharmila and I know our ministry has flourished much more by being connected in the Body of Christ. There is a place of blessing and supernatural covering that exists when we are in a place of fellowship and submission to one another (see Ephesians 5:21).

When we are in fellowship with each other, our ceiling becomes the floor for the next generation. Pastor Bill Johnson of Bethel Church in Redding, California models this better than any other person I have ever met. This church believes in raising up and equipping the next generation all over the world and gives the next generation the tools and opportunities to release this through team ministry and various ministry opportunities. As we travel often to India, Nepal and German speaking nations we regularly see Pastor Bill's influence and how this mindset has spread worldwide. In fellowship we train up and release others for effective ministry. This causes the Gospel to multiply.

The centurion also understood that we have been given

authority. If we are to perform the miracles Jesus performed, we need to look at how He used His authority (given to all mankind, to those born here) along with the power of Holy Spirit to command sickness, infirmities, and demons to go. Every person born on planet earth was given authority. What they do with that authority is another thing. Believers just like Jesus; need the Holy Spirit to help us carry out our authority. *How God anointed Jesus of Nazareth with the Holy Spirit and with power, who went about doing good and healing all who were oppressed by the devil, for God was with Him* (Acts 10:38). Many were awed by the authority that Jesus operated in. Don't just be awed by it, thinking you can never do the things He did. He modeled it for us to show us we can do the same. We have the same authority available to us because the same Holy Spirit is living in us. We just need to learn from Jesus' example of how to operate in authority. He set the pattern we are to follow.

For now [in this time of imperfection] we see in a mirror dimly [a blurred reflection, a riddle, an enigma], but then [when the time of perfection comes we will see reality] face to face. **Now I know in part [just in fragments]**, *but then I will know fully, just as I have been fully known [by God]* (1 Corinthians 13:12 Amp). Some will try to explain away the authority of mankind based on negative experiences. As the above verse states we now only see in part or in fragments. Just because I can't explain or understand some circumstances in life does not change God's Word in the least. This is where faith kicks in and we trust God even when we can't understand or see clearly what we are facing. This also is a reason we come together and we lean on each other because each person has his part of the puzzle and together we can put that puzzle together and see a move of God, if we work together.

Don't let negative experiences make you compromise what God says in His Word. You have authority over negative things in this life. *Trust in and rely confidently on the Lord with all your heart And do not rely on your own insight or understanding. In all your ways know and acknowledge and recognize Him, And He will make your paths straight and smooth [removing obstacles that block your way]* (Proverbs 3:5-6 Amp).

Munshi Lal - was in a severe accident 1 1/2 years ago. A metal rod was installed. He was in great pain and asked the doctor about removing it that day. The cost was too much. During prayer time Mark said "Jesus is dissolving metal." He was healed and came forward to demonstrate - **Ballabgarh, India February 25, 2014.**

CHAPTER 9

Testimonies Release Confidence And Authority

...For the testimony of Jesus is the spirit of prophecy (Revelation 19:10). When we begin to share the testimonies of Jesus we are prophesying that He is able to do the same miracles again and again. **The word testimony in Hebrew means to do again.** This principle has worked successfully in our overseas campaigns as we share testimonies of the healings Jesus has done in previous campaigns. As people hear these testimonies their faith is quickened to believe Jesus for a similar miracle for themselves. Testimonies of what God has done in your life can give you authority, confidence and empowerment. It also can empower others to do the same, as they see Holy Spirit work through you. The testimonies of Jesus are contagious.

God anointed Moses' rod to do miracles. *Then Moses*

137

answered and said, "But suppose they will not believe me or listen to my voice; suppose they say, 'The Lord has not appeared to you.'"So the Lord said to him, "What is that in your hand?" He said, "A rod."And He said, "Cast it on the ground." So he cast it on the ground, and it became a serpent; and Moses fled from it. Then the Lord said to Moses, "Reach out your hand and take it by the tail" (and he reached out his hand and caught it, and it became a rod in his hand) (Exodus 4:1-4). Moses ended up operating with great confidence and authority whenever he cast his rod on the ground in Pharaoh's presence. Why was that? He heard God say He would do miracles through that rod and saw God perform miracles when he used his rod. Miracles, signs and wonders took place each time. So many undeniable miracles, signs and wonders took place that Pharaoh had no choice but to let all of Israel go free. The testimonies of what God had done earlier gave Moses confidence and authority that next time he cast it on the ground miracles would happen again. His rod became a scepter of authority and power.

We operate on this principle in ministry. Whenever we have seen Holy Spirit confirm God's Word with a sign, wonder, miracle or healing it gives us great confidence and authority to perform and repeat those same things again and again. Once I started seeing metal dissolve in people's bodies I just came to expect God would do it again, and sure enough, He has done it many times both in the USA and overseas. It is the same with cancer, tumors, crippled bodies, broken bones, demons, blindness, deafness, severe back problems, you name it. We have seen so many people healed just by sharing the testimonies of what God has done in the past. Now every time I minister in large open air outreaches in north India and Nepal I begin the first night by mostly sharing testimonies of what Jesus has done in our previous meetings.

Let me share about one of those times. We saw very powerful, undeniable, and unusual miracles and healings in our **Ghaziabad, Utter Pradesh, India** November 1-5, 2011 outreach. Most leaders there thought our outreach would be small because this city was known as one of the crime capitals of India and there had never been a successful outreach there before. Because of the powerful miracles from the the first night onwards the crowd grew in size and thousands came out to hear about Jesus. I decided to try an experiment on our next outreach which was in **Kohalpur, Nepal** April 3-5, 2012, where we saw about 4,700 people come to Christ. I decided each night I would share some undeniable and strange miracles and healings that occurred in Ghaziabad and see if Holy Spirit will repeat them in Kohalpur. I also thought of other strange or different testimonies to share there that we had seen Holy Spirit do. When sharing these testimonies in Kohalpur I felt an authority and confidence that whatever I shared about, Holy Spirit would repeat those that very day. Sure enough He did!

Below is an article by Sharmila Anderson in our Fall 2011 Good News Magazine that best describes what Jesus did in **Ghaziabad, India (markanderson-wpengine.netdna-ssl. com/wp-content/uploads/2013/04/images1/magazine-fall-2011.pdf).**

"Please do not stop telling people about Jesus. Go all over and tell people about Him." This urgent plea was made to us by **Ram Pyari**, a 65-70 year old woman who attended the campaign in **Ghaziabad**. Standing on the stage she boldly took the microphone from Mark and testified in front of thousands, *"I have just heard about Jesus. What a lovely name! He has healed my body and I am experiencing such peace and joy.* **I wonder what my life and the life of my children would have been like if I had heard about Him earlier."** In one sense these are chilling words to hear. Are we doing enough to reach out to the unreached? **Will we reach them before it's eternally too late?** We can always do more and our desire is to do more! However as we consider the fruit of this outreach and the number of lives that were touched, healed and changed Mark and I know that we are exactly where God desires us to be at this time and also that our heart in reaching out to the remote areas is on target.

Upon arrival in Ghaziabad we learned that this city is a major crime capital in India. For this reason the advertising for the campaign was very low key. Mark and I have discovered that we don't really need any major advertising. Once Jesus arrives on the scene and begins to perform miracles the word spreads like wild fire and people attend from all over. The spiritual condition of the area does not stop Him. This is exactly what happened in Ghaziabad, India November 1-5, 2011. We truly experienced an open heaven. On the first night an 11-year-old boy, **Shivam** who was crippled from birth (with polio) walked for the first time in his life. Yeah Jesus! This set the atmosphere for the miraculous.

Bala, a 50-year-old lady, suffered with severe pain as her uterus had shifted and was protruding out of her body. She could not sit and had great difficulty in going to the toilet. She had suffered with this for a very long time. Being a poor women she could not afford medical treatment. During mass prayer she felt an invisible hand push her uterus back in place. After testifying she remained on the stage. We continued to interview other people about their healings. I noticed Bala raise her hands and begin to worship Jesus with tears streaming down her cheek; pretty soon she was speaking in tongues. A few minutes later Mark shouts out that he could understand her as she was speaking in English. There is no way this illiterate villager could speak in English. It was the Holy Spirit all over her. She was praising and thanking Jesus in English.

Every night several testified that they received instant healings as they either saw angels, lightening, felt electric currents or felt an invisible hand touch them. **Monica** testified on the final night of the campaign of the healing she received the night before. She had a huge cyst in her stomach. During mass prayer she began to bleed severely. She thought she was going to die. Later at home as she changed her blood soaked clothes she found the cyst in her undergarments. She felt wonderful the next day and testified of her miracle.

The list of people who found freedom from demonic torment, healed of cancers, asthma, epilepsy, polio, deafness, blindness goes on and on... Jesus is truly unstoppable! We estimate that approximately 6,000 people made a first time decision for Jesus in Ghaziabad. We have been in touch with pastors from Ghaziabad who have been telling us that almost every participating church has grown after the campaign. Our main contact says that a stronghold has been broken in Ghaziabad as a result of this outreach and people are flocking into the Kingdom.

Here is part of article I wrote in our *Spring 2012 Good News Magazine (markanderson-wpengine.netdna-ssl.com/*

wp-content/uploads/2012/05/spring-2012-magazine-web.pdf) that best describes what happened in **Kohalpur, Nepal** as testimonies from our **Ghaziabad, India** outreach were shared.

Revelation 19:10 says *"...For the testimony of Jesus is the spirit of prophecy."* Whenever you and I share the miracle testimonies of Jesus we prophecy that He will repeat those testimonies. Each day I shared about the many powerful miracles Jesus has done in our meetings around the world. Each testimony I shared, no matter how different or unusual, brought about the same healings and miracles during mass prayer, along with many other powerful miracles. All I can say is don't stop proclaiming Jesus and His awesome deeds!

During the last night of the Kohalpur campaign (with an estimated crowd of 3,800), we saw the most healings. We waited on Holy Spirit and let Him sweep through the crowd with no hands being laid on anyone. Many undeniable miracles took place this night. At the same time bizarre witchcraft activity occurred, unlike anything I have seen before in my travels. Suddenly while Holy Spirit was healing many, strong winds and dark clouds came out of nowhere. It looked like it was going to pour rain but I rebuked it and it stayed dry. Because of the strong winds dust began to cover the area where we were praying a mass prayer and waiting on the Holy Spirit. That is when many were instantly healed by Jesus. We have heard that each of the 30 participating churches in the Kohalpur campaign (mostly village churches) have added anywhere from 15 up to 50 new members in their churches since the campaign.

Here are just a few of the testimonies I shared in Kohalpur, Nepal, of Holy Spirit healing people of identical problems. Check out our youtube video of this outreach: **Miracle Healings in Kohalpur, Nepal (*www.markandersonministries. com/videos/miracle-healings-in-kohalpur-nepal*).** I shared Bala's testimony of an invisible hand putting her uterus back in place. A lady came up after prayer that day who said the exact same thing happened to her and her uterus was healed.

I shared about Shivam, 11 years old, who had polio, and was crippled from birth, how Jesus healed him the first night and he walked on the stage. Many cripples in Kohalpur were also instantly healed including Maan Bhadar Magar who was paralyzed for seven years and had not walked a step. He was carried on a cot to the outreach. After prayer that closing day he got up off his cot and walked to the front, with the crowd screaming for joy. I shared that Jesus was opening blind eyes in India and many blind people were instantly healed and demonstrated they could see clearly. One was a young boy who was almost totally blind since birth but after mass prayer was instantly healed by Jesus and could see clearly. Another was Maan Bhadari who was totally blind for 12 years.

I shared one day about a number of people Jesus had healed of cancer and tumors and many who had tumors and cancer were healed that day. One Bible passage I read in most of our outreaches in India and Nepal is about the story of the woman who suffered with an issue of blood for 12 years (see Mark 25-34). When she touched the hem of Jesus garment virtue went out and she was instantly healed. So many times in India we have read this story and many women have been instantly healed of the same problem. One of those ladies, Rekha from Malerkotla, Punjab, India was healed while reading the story of Jesus healing the woman with the issue of blood. By the way Malerkotla is the former hometown of Louisiana's former Governor Bobby Jindal's parents. I share this story about Rekha often. After sharing this story in Kohalpur we prayed a mass prayer for the crowd that gathered for healing. A woman came up afterwards and said she had an issue of blood and suffered for 12 years with her problem. Exactly the same number of years as the woman healed in Mark 5:25-34. After prayer she was instantly healed. The more we share this testimony the more we see women healed of the same problem time and time again. It has become one of the most common healings in our outreaches to India and Nepal.

One other testimony I shared in Kohalpur was of Carmen who was healed in a meeting we did in Wyoming, Minnesota,

USA many years ago. Her gall bladder had been surgically removed. During our meeting in Wyoming the power of God hit her and she was given a brand new gall bladder by Dr. Jesus. She went back to the same doctor who just days earlier had removed the gall bladder and had him do an X-ray. The doctor confirmed she had been given a brand new gall bladder by Jesus. That day in Kohalpur I believed Jesus would heal gall bladders and dissolve stones. After mass prayer for healing, one lady testified that Jesus had healed her gall bladder by dissolving the stones, healed her heart, and also severe headaches all at once. A man also came up and testified the stones he had in his kidneys for eleven years were instantly dissolved. There is power and authority released in sharing the testimonies of our great God. It creates an atmosphere of faith for miracles and healings where Holy Spirit repeats the same miracles and healings time and time again.

Jesus Heals At Two Deaf Schools In North India

After doing a rock and roll concert on the school grounds, where we were conducting our evening campaign in Ghaziabad, India, I was asked if I would share at the deaf and mute school on the same grounds, to about 70 students. This was the first time I have preached through someone using sign language. I shared how much Jesus loved these students and that He treats all equally. I shared testimonies of the healings Jesus was doing in the evening, how he was opening deaf ears and that He could open their deaf ears. I asked how many wanted prayer to have their ears open. All raised their hands. I went through the line and prayed over each student commanding a deaf and mute spirit to go in Jesus' name. Afterwards I asked how many could hear. Half of the students raised their hands! Check it out on YouTube: **Jesus heals at Deaf School Ghaziabad, India** *www.markandersonministries.com/videos/jesus-heals-at-deaf-dumb-school-ghaziabad-india.* Later that evening a number of these children who were healed of deafness came to the evening outreach where they testified and demonstrated that they could hear now that Jesus had opened their ears.

The testimonies of Jesus prophesy that Jesus can do it again. A short time after being in the Ghaziabad deaf and mute school where thirty to forty students were healed we were in Roorkee, India doing an outreach and a school concert. Word about what Jesus had done in Ghaziabad spread and I was asked to speak at a deaf and mute school in Roorkee. While conducting our outreach in Roorkee the most outstanding miracles we saw were at the **deaf school in Roorkee.** I shared with these kids that Jesus loved them, about the Ghaziabad school and that Jesus was performing miracles and opening deaf ears. I asked if any of them desired prayer for healing. All of them raised their hands.

Our team of five laid hands on every kid. Three of those with me at the school were from Norway. At first they were laying hands on the children and nothing was happening. I told them to lay hands on their ears, take authority over the deaf and mute spirit, command it to go and move on to the next child. I told them just know your words have authority and even if you do not see anything happen know things are happening. Don't stay stuck on one child. Sure enough they moved on that word and went right down the line and we also did the same with our lines of children. After we finished laying hands on these children and taking authority in Jesus name I asked "how many of you can hear now?" About 70 out of 80 kids were healed by Jesus.

Many demonstrated they could hear us clap behind them as we tested their hearing. Then they wanted me to sing songs knowing I was a singer and had just performed a concert earlier that morning at a local school. The smiles on their faces was priceless. They loved hearing music (songs about Jesus) for the first time in their life. Afterwards all the children prayed to receive Jesus as their Lord. All of this was caught on video. We uploaded it on **youtube**. It is titled *Jesus heals at deaf School in Northern India   www.markandersonministries.com/videos/ jesus-heals-at-deaf-school-in-northern-india.*

Since this Roorkee outreach the power of the testimony

continues to multiply. We had the privilege of having Oyvind and Hilde Haereid from Norway join us on multiple trips to India and Nepal. Both of them are retired from their jobs. Oyvind was a public school principal and Hilde was a nurse. Whenever they join us many miracles and healings take place as they lay hands on people. In one outreach in Nepal not many healings and miracles were taking place until Oyvind and Hilde started laying hands on deaf people. Many deaf people were healed and as a result the faith of the people there soared and many more miracles and healings broke out. Ever since praying over the deaf and mute students in Roorkee this couple walks in a tremendous authority and confidence in the area of healing and miracles especially when praying for the deaf. Now they are busy traveling to many countries each year, teaching and training workers for healing and deliverance ministry.

Saroj - saw bright lightning in sky. Knee healed! - **Ghaziabad, Utttar Pradesh, India November 2011.**

Bala - Illiterate village woman! Overcome with tears after she felt an invisible hand during mass prayer put her uterus back into place in body. Afterwards while standing on the stage she was baptized in the Holy Spirit and began speaking tongues in English - **Ghaziabad, Utttar Pradesh, India November 2, 2011.**

Shivam - Born cripple! So happy to walk for the first time in his life right after Jesus heals him - **Ghaziabad November 1, 2011.**

Monica - A huge cyst passed out of her body and she was instantly healed - **Ghaziabad November 4, 2011.**

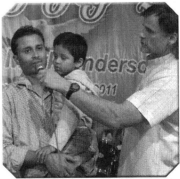

This man was in a severe motorcycle accident. He could only lift 5 lbs. Healed by Jesus! Lifts his son - **Ghaziabad November 3, 2011.**

Pastors and leaders who attended our 3 day training conference in **Kohalpur, Nepal April 2012.**

After praying over deaf and mute students many testified they could hear! Ingraham Deaf and Mute School - **Ghaziabad, Uttar Pradesh, India November 4, 2011.**

Young girl demonstrates she can hear clapping after Jesus opens her deaf ears at a Deaf School, along with many other classmates - **Roorkee, Uttarakhand, India November 8, 2012.**

Maan Bhadari - One of many blind who received their sight back after Jesus opened her eyes. She had been blind for 12 years - **Kohalpur, Nepal April 4, 2012.**

Maan Bhadar Magar - Man who was paralyzed for 7 years was carried to the campaign, walks on his own after Jesus healed him during mass prayer - **Kohalpur, Nepal April 5, 2012.**

On the last day of **Kohalpur, Nepal** campaign many come forward during mass prayer for healing. Many were instantly healed as we waited on the presence of the Holy Spirit to move - **April 5, 2012.**

This man was ecstatic showing us his x-rays and medical records. He had been paralyzed in his upper legs and experiencing great pain in his lower legs. Instantly healed by Jesus - **Kohalpur, Nepal April 5, 2012.**

This young man was coming home from work when he heard our meeting going on and came in to see what was happening. He did not know what drew him there. He stayed and was healed of a serious heart condition and asthma - **New Delhi, India April 12, 2012.**

This woman could not bend her arm because of a rod in her arm. After prayer by one lady and a 14 yr. old girl she was able to bend her arm. Either Jesus dissolved the rod or made it very bendable!!! **New Delhi, India outreach April 12, 2012.**

This woman heard me share about a woman in Ghaziabad, India who felt an invisible hand go into her body and put her uterus back into place in November 2011. That day when we she received prayer the exact same thing happened to her uterus- **Kohalpur, Nepal April 2012.**

Hukum - born crippled! Never walked until Jesus healed him during worship time - **Chamba, India June 2, 2011.**

CONCLUSION

Heaven's Health assurance Policy

This teaching is not just something that sounds like a good teaching to share around the world but it is something we live on a personal basis as well. Jesus the Healer has taken great care of me. At the time of writing this book I turned 60 years old. I have never had health insurance in my life. Nor have I needed it. Am I against having health insurance? No! My daughter Charisma had health insurance and we were grateful she did at times. For me personally I have never needed it. Have I been ill or have I had an injury? Yes! But for me something that has worked way better than very expensive health insurance is the '**Heavenly Health Assurance Policy**' that God gives us through His Word. Sharmila and I live believing in the health assurance that comes through God's Word and by His grace.

In the 23 years of our marriage the only time Sharmila had

a health insurance plan was when she was pregnant with our daughter Charisma. It definitely came in handy during those days. We needed it! So don't go cancel your health insurance because of what I say. That is not what I am getting at. We thank God for His grace that has kept us healthy and walking in divine health as we travel to many countries each year. Heaven has been working on our behalf to keep us healthy. Year after year of seeing His goodness to us regarding our health and divine healing, we walk in a confidence and authority He will continue to keep us healthy or heal us. We had to start by trusting Him and His Word in order to see this take place. We put in to practice what we have been writing about in this book.

I'm not sharing this to say look at us or to say do the same as us, but I am writing this to give glory to God. When people saw Jesus heal, many times they gave glory to God. God is glorified when people are healed and delivered by His power. I am sharing this to say look at our great God, our healer, protector, and the authority He has given us through His Word. When you live by His Word and put faith in His grace it works. Keep in mind Sharmila and I do our part and believe in exercise. In fact Sharmila believes in a lot of exercise and somehow I do too because she pushes me in that area, always challenging me to do more than I thought I could! We also believe in eating right, taking some vitamins, juicing and proper rest. I know for a fact if we did not do these things we would not be so healthy. There are physical laws and there are spiritual laws when it comes to healing and walking in divine health. Be in tune to both the physical and spiritual realms. Some ignore one realm and pay the price with poor health. I share a lot about this in my book **OVERCOMING ROADBLOCKS TO HEALING.**

I do not believe somehow Sharmila and I are the special ones and that is how we stay healed and healthy. We do our part in the natural and also trust God. I do believe *God* ***shows personal favoritism to no man*** (Galatians 2:6). *For God shows no partiality [no arbitrary favoritism; with Him one person is not more important than another]* (Romans 2:11 Amp). If God does this for Sharmila and I, He can also keep you healthy. Learn about your authority, how it operates, and stand firmly on what His Word says regarding healing and health. We do our part in this natural realm to take care of our bodies, which are the temples of the Holy Spirit, but we also know that God has done a lot to keep us healthy. We are so very grateful and express that to Him on a regular basis.

Let me share a story of every day life. Sharmila and I have had an occasional cold and had to trust God for healing for small things like that. We have had some minor aches and pains from traveling abroad or working out a lot at the gym and received healing from Jesus or help for those aches. We do thank God for our close friend Dr. Paul Bergamini, one our board members, a missionary, who is a very good chiropractor and nutritionist in Cody. Dr. Paul also edits our books for us. He has adjusted us on a few occasions and we feel a lot better. One injury I have had on two occasions, and was healed supernaturally of, was a rotator cuff injury. Over the years I have enjoyed playing Men's City League Flag Football. One of my weaknesses is I love football. I have played quarterback and receiver in a Canadian Mens League while living in Lethbridge, Alberta, and played other positions as well here in the USA. I also coached my son Reed's Pee Wee football team for 3 years. Playing and coaching football was a lot of fun!

Standing in Authority

While playing men's city league football in Kalispell, Montana in a playoff game, I was playing defense. I was chasing the guy running with the football and out of the corner of my eye I saw a guy flying at me, to block me. I went flying through the air as he clipped me on the side and I tore my rotator cuff. I was in a lot of pain and could not even move my arm up. I went off the field, went home and had my two young sons pray over me. They prayed and asked Jesus to heal their daddy. Cute prayer! I was a single parent in those days and framed houses for a living. After prayer I thanked God for healing. I believe what Jesus said in Mark 11:23-24 (Amplified). *I assure you and most solemnly say to you, whoever says to this mountain, 'Be lifted up and thrown into the sea!' and does not doubt in his heart [in God's **unlimited power**], but believes that what he says is going to take place, it will be done for him [in accordance with God's will]. For this reason I am telling you, whatever things* *you ask for in prayer [in accordance with God's will], believe [with confident trust] that you have received them, and they will be given to you.* I know healing is His will because He paid a terrible price to obtain healing for all of us when He was headed to the cross. One of the best ways to believe you receive something from God is to praise Him for that or to confess what His word says about your circumstance. I do not ignore the problem either. That is not how the problem leaves.

I went to work the next day and could hardly lift my hammer to pound nails, let alone lift the walls we were framing. Despite the pain I kept speaking God's word concerning healing over my body like *By His stripes I am healed* (1 Peter 2:24) and how He sent His word and healed me (see Psalms 107:20). Nothing happened right after my boys prayed for me but within 48 hours I was 100% healed and could do anything on the job site, including lifting heavy walls that we framed. A number of people I have met who had rotator cuff injuries had to have surgery and it took many months to recover. Standing on His word and using the authority I have in Jesus name took only 48 hours for complete healing to manifest itself in my shoulder.

My main position when I played High School and Junior College football was kicker. A very safe position when it comes to **tackle** football, especially if you are just skin and bones, like I was in High School. 6'2", 145lbs! I still go out and kick the football occasionally. Recently my right knee was healed by standing on God's Word. I had been prayed over time and time again. Sometimes I would get healed and the problem would surface again. This minor knee problem lingered for several years and really restricted me in some ways from being as mobile as I would have liked. On one occasion I was writing an article on **Laying an Unshakable Foundation for Healing** in our **Winter 2014 Good News Magazine** (*www.markanderson-wpengine.netdna-ssl. com/wp-content/uploads/2014/03/winter-2014-magazine-web.pdf*). The day I wrote it and was studying this out I went to the gym and rode a stationary bike for long time. When I finished biking I got off and felt my leg was almost 100% healed, with great flexibility. I gave all praises to God and was so happy. I figured the best way to test this out would be to go the local Cody High School football field and kick some field goals. I had Sharmila come along and record it on video. Thanks to the Lord's healing power I was able to kick multiple 47 yard field goals that day. My leg and knee felt great! Check our youtube video Mark's Personal Testimony of Knee Healing *www.markandersonministries.com/ videos/marks-personal-testimony-knee-healing.* Thank God for our God-given authority and the promise of healing and divine health found in His Word.

God gave each one of us authority in the beginning of time. What happens if we do not use that authority? Look at what happened to Adam and Eve and all mankind when they did not use their authority, but instead submitted to Satan's lies and handed over their authority to him. Look at the heartache, death, destruction, sin, evil that has flourished because they did not use their God-given authority even though God gave them authority over *everything that creeps on the earth* (Genesis 1:26). Satan came in the form of a serpent creeping on the earth, yet Adam did not exercise authority over him. In these last days will you rise up and use the authority God gave you or will you or be one who submits to Satan's plan for your life and resists God's plan?

Theresa Stoner understood what it was to resist the enemy when she was afflicted with lymphatic cancer. In April of 2002 I was asked to conduct a healing service at Faith Heights Church in Grand Junction, Colorado. Theresa came to the healing service that night. In Theresa's words *"That night Mark called for those who needed healing in specific areas to come up and I was one of the first. He had said the Holy Spirit had told him someone with my problem* (lymphatic cancer) *was there. He and Sharmila laid hands on me, and the Holy Spirit moved mightily to heal me. The pressure left my neck and throat. I felt energy I had not had in a long time. For the rest*

Theresa Stoner - Came forward after a word of knowledge was given that someone needed to be healed of lymphatic cancer. She received instant healing from Christ, the enemy tried several times to put it back on her but she resisted and was completely healed- **Faith Heights Church- Grand Junction, Colorado April 14, 2002.**

of the service I felt as though I had gravel draining down my throat and that pressure was being lifted from all over my head, neck, and shoulders. I was filled with joy and freedom. I wanted to dance."

After being healed supernaturally by God the enemy tried to attack her with the cancer again. In Theresa's own words: *"The devil, several times starting the next day, put symptoms of pressure on my throat, stabs of pain, etc, but I was quick to rebuke him and the symptoms left. I never expected Mark and Sharmila to be in my church that Sunday. He moved miraculously through their anointed ministry to preserve my life for His glory, my family's needs and my joy.* Pastor John Cappetto has laid a good foundation in his church for healing and how to stand for healing. Knowing these things, Theresa stood her ground and resisted the devil's plan to afflict her with cancer again.

Theresa understood that sometimes faith is a fight and fought the fight of faith for her life and healing. She came out victoriously in Jesus' name. God will do the same for you if you do not passively give into the attacks of the enemy, but withstand or resist him. Once again James 4:7 says *Submit to God. Resist the devil and he will flee from you.*

While building our home/ministry office in Cody in 2001 I re-injured my rotator cuff from continual heavy lifting of logs and walls. I had already received a miraculous healing of this before in the early 1990s. I received prayer for the problem but there seemed to be little change this time, even though last time I was healed within 48 hours of being prayed for. Finally at a Peter Youngren meeting in Denver, Colorado, I was completely healed when Peter called out a word of knowledge for my exact problem. I returned home and lifted heavy things over my head with no problem. I threw the football to my son with no problem. I played basketball and could shoot the ball with no discomfort.

A short time after my healing I was playing basketball and my shoulder felt great. My game was far from great though. However, while I was playing, the symptoms returned and I could feel the pain again. I quickly rebuked the enemy while running down the court and said you are not taking my healing away. I confessed God's word and immediately I was healed again. Since that day, I have had no problem whatsoever with my shoulder.

Many give up on healing if the problems return because they have not learned to stand in authority when the enemy tries a counter attack. Speak God's Word and stand for what rightfully belongs to you through Christ and watch God's Word work. In Matthew 24:35, Jesus said *Heaven and earth will pass away, but My words will by no means pass away.* You have authority because of what Christ has done. Use it! Don't become passive and submit to the Devil's plan. Submit to God's plan for your life and health and watch Him come through. Heaven backs His Word. No devil or demon can prevent His Word from coming to pass. *He who is in you is greater than he who is in the world* (1 John 4:4). When we stand on His Word all heaven backs it up. Your words have power. When you speak and confess God's Word with a heart full of faith you can change your negative circumstances. Time to rise up my friend! Start using your God-given authority, partner with heaven and Holy Spirit, and help change this world for the better. Use your authority for the good of mankind. Don't sit on it, but learn how to effectively release heaven wherever you go. You can do it in His name and many will come to Christ.

SALVATION PRAYER

If you do not know Jesus as Lord and Savior take the time to invite Him into your life right now. Romans 10:9-10 says *that if you confess with your mouth the Lord Jesus and believe in your heart that God has raised Him from the dead, you will be saved. For with the heart one believes unto righteousness, and with the mouth confession is made unto salvation. Pray this simple prayer today: Jesus I believe you died for me and were raised from the dead. Come into my life. Be my Lord and my Savior. Forgive my sins. I will live for you, because you died for me. I trust you for my salvation and that you will give me eternal life. I pray this in Jesus' name.* Amen! Pray that from your heart and you will be saved!

War veterans healed! **Fred Cox** (L) - saw a multi-colored flash and was instantly delivered of a demon and deafness. **Joe Johnson** (R) Healed of 48 years of deafness and knee problems - **Crescent City, CA April 2000.**

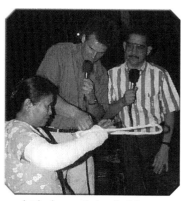

Lady demonstrates that Jesus healed her broken arm- **Nagarote, Nicaragua February 1993.**

Memory - had injured her right leg 4 times and was on crutches. Holy Spirit shrunk her right leg back to normal. Completely healed! **Savoonga, (St. Lawerence Island) Alaska April 26, 2011.**

Dolly Petroff - had a severe hernia and was on many meds for 18 years. After prayer went to washroom and passed something from her body. Afterwards she weighed herself. 35 lbs lighter and healed! **Toronto, Canada January 12, 1997.**

EXCELLENT BOOKS ON THIS SUBJECT

Christianity Unshackled
by Harold R. Eberle
*worldcastministries.
com/books/christianity-
unshackled.*

Schizophrenic God?
by Steve C. Shank
www.stevecshank.com

or

*www.markandersonministries.
com/product/schizophrenic-god.*

ENDNOTES

Chapter 2

3. Augustine, Enchiridion, 395.

4. Augustine, City of God 5.10; Nicene and Post-Nicene Fathers, First Series, ed. Alexander Roberts, James Donaldson, Philip Schaff, and Henry Wace, 14 vols. (Peabody, MA: Hendrickson Publishers, 1994), 2:93.

5. John Calvin, Institutes of the Christian Religion, ed. James T. McNeill, trans. Ford L. Battles (Philadelphia: Westminster Press, 1960), pp. 198-199 [1.16.2].

6. Justin Martyr, 2 Apology 5; The Ante-Nicene Fathers, ed. A. Roberts and J. Donaldson, 10 vols. (Grand Rapids, MI: Eerdmans, 1979), 1:190.

7. Ibid.

8. Clement of Alexandria, Stromata 1.17; Roberts and Donaldson, op. cit., 2:319.

9. Tertullian, Apology 22; Roberts and Donaldson, op. cit., 3:36.

10. Tertullian, Exhortation on Chastity 2; Roberts and Donaldson, op. cit., 4:50-51.

11. Origen, Against Celsus 4.65; Roberts and Donaldson, op. cit., 4:527.

12. John Calvin and John T. McNeill (ed) Institutes of the Christian religion, Volume 1, Book, (Westminster John Knox Press, Louisville, KY, 2008), p.200

Chapter 4

1   Wikipedia April 2015 Nepal earthquake

2   Wikipedia Gadhimai festival

Chapter 7

1- *www.christiancourier.com/articles/1-meet-ted-turner-thanks-id-rather-not*

2- *www.mrmediatraining.com/2011/03/09/jesus-freaks-a-ted-turner-ash-wednesday*

3- *www.christianpost.com/news/cnn-founder-ted-turner-talks-prayer-heaven-hell-108968*

Mark and Sharmila Anderson

Vision:

Reaching the unreached, telling the untold, churching the unchurched and training Christians to reach the unreached.

How:

Through open-air campaigns, ministry training conferences, women's conferences (with Sharmila Anderson), planting churches, supporting national ministry leaders, orphanages, literature, CD distribution and rock music.

Main Focus:

Rural and unreached areas.

Mark Anderson has been sharing the gospel, conducting campaigns, singing and planting churches since 1978. Over 200,000 people have already responded to Christ in his overseas campaigns. Churches have been planted from campaigns in India and Bulgaria. Mark has also helped pioneer churches in Canada and the United States.

Mark and his wife, Sharmila, travel together, fulfilling the Great Commission. Sharmila is also a very gifted teacher. Her main area of ministry has been training women to be all they can be in Christ.

To have Mark & Sharmila Anderson come speak in your area or for more information about Mark Anderson Ministries and a list of Mark's books and teaching CDs, please contact them at:

Mark Anderson Ministries
P.O. Box 66
Cody, WY 82414-0066 USA
www.markandersonministries.com
E-mail us at: goodnews@vcn.com
Phone: 307-587-0408

For other books by Mark Anderson, please visit their website:
www.markandersonministries.com/store

OVERCOMING ROADBLOCKS TO HEALING

—— Mark R. Anderson ——

Published by Apostolic Network of Global Awakening in 2012

Have you ever received prayer for healing or deliverance and nothing seemed to happen or you were healed only to lose your healing or deliverance a short time later? In this book we search out answers from God's Word to reveal things that can hinder healing. Clear cut answers from God's Word show how to overcome roadblocks to healing or deliverance.

Mark Anderson shares many things from his years of experience in the healing ministry. He explores major hindrances to miracles, healings and deliverance in western Christianity. Many Christians do not realize just how much Greek Philosophy influences their everyday Christian walk and belief system when it comes to healings and miracles.

In this book he explores what was Paul's Thorn in the flesh with scriptures and also examines the view that had it roots in Greek Philosophy. How to properly stand for healing, a miracle or deliverance is addressed. The final two chapters show how people like you and I overcame huge roadblocks to their healing and received their miracle from Jesus. You to can overcome the roadblocks to healing.

"Overcoming Roadblocks to Healing is an outstanding practical guide for those who are struggling to understand why healing does not come or last. At times, you may think the prayer of faith has failed or that you have done something to cause your sickness or pain to return. You may not know what to do next. I have been praying for the sick for many years. I have seen God do mighty things when praying for someone one time and then not see any results when praying for someone else another time. I have experienced victories and defeats in my own healing ministry and struggled at times with the mystery of why some do not get healed.

I believe Mark provides key insights from Scripture to help those who come against roadblocks in their healing. He not only offers strategy to get your healing, but gives personal experience where he has struggled to be healed or at times lost his healing. He tells you the truth about his struggle and the victory of overcoming his roadblocks to healing.

Mark exposes the lies that have caused believers to deny that healing exists or that it is not for today. He reveals the influence of Greek thought on our Western Christianity, which has caused a false belief that suffering and illness are the will of God for our lives. This misunderstanding has caused many to doubt that God can heal and their unwillingness to seek healing for their illness. Mark emphasizes that the truth of God's Word is the standard for which we should put our faith in. He stresses the need for believers to renew their minds by aligning thoughts and beliefs with the Word of God.

I believe this book should be read by every believer, especially those who need healing. It is a tremendous resource for those who have not walked in the healing ministry, to be aware of roadblocks in people's lives to healing. Thank you, Mark, for providing such a wonderful book that will help the church understand how to overcome the roadblocks to healing. "

– Randy Clark, Apostolic Network of Global Awakening

HUMILITY: THE HIDDEN KEYS TO WALKING IN SIGNS AND WONDERS

—— Mark R. Anderson ——

Originally published by Destiny Image in 2010

Humility is the basis for spiritual and personal breakthrough—no matter your present circumstances. A fresh look at a trait that God welcomes and richly rewards.

As a teacher in the United States and to Third World countries, author Mark Anderson has observed first-hand how pride can destroy people and churches, while humility can revive and refresh people—and energize and expand even a fledgling ministry.

When pride comes, then comes shame; but with the humble is wisdom (Proverbs 11:2 NKJV).

Humility The Hidden Key to Walking in Signs and Wonders reveals the conflict between arrogance and humility and explores the fruits of this often-neglected but wholly vital virtue.

"The enemy would love for us to neglect humility because of its importance in ushering in the greatest move of God this world has seen," writes the author, who has spent 34 years sharing the gospel worldwide.

"This book helps you navigate your life between blatant pride and false humility helping you recognize what true humility looks like...The book is like a diamond in that humility is the diamond, and Mark helps us see all the various facets of the diamond, and there were many, all of which I found very helpful...

Humility the Hidden Key to Walking in Signs and Wonders, is the best book I have ever read on humility, and reveals the importance of humility's relationship to spiritual breakthrough, and revival."

– Randy Clark

YOU CAN TAP INTO CHRIST'S HEALING POWER

— Mark R. Anderson —

Published by Mark Anderson Ministries 2004

Miracles and healings do not have to be a rarity in your life or the life of any Spirit-filled or Spirit-led believer. By understanding your God-given authority and how to partner with the Holy Spirit, You can tap into Christ's healing power!

Christ made a show of the enemy openly. You can enforce what He accomplished 2,000 years ago. Sometimes faith is a fight. Learn how to stand for what rightfully belongs to you in Christ. Learn how your words shape and affect the way you live your life.

By understanding something that the children of Israel understood, you can create an atmosphere conducive for the Holy Spirit to move in power. You can literally affect the spiritual realm, releasing Christ's healing power in this physical realm. Learn the role humility will play in the healing ministry in these last days.

"Healing the sick was front and center in Jesus ministry. Mark Anderson has years of practical experience in seeing people receive miraculous healing through faith in Christ. His book You Can Tap Into Christ's Healing Power lays a foundation for healing and sets an atmosphere where miracles can easily be received. This teaching is for those who need healing for themselves, as well as for the one who wants to minister God's healing life to others."

– Evangelist Peter Youngren
St. Catherines, Ontario, Canada

SOUL WINNING: GOD'S HEARTBEAT

— Mark R. Anderson —

Published by Mark Anderson Ministries 2000

Do you have the desire to reach the lost? Then this book is for you. It includes discussion of:

- Witnessing with a passion for souls

- Overcoming the fear of witnessing

- Successful evangelism keys

- Prayerful spiritual warfare and insight into the spirit realm

- Saying the right things at the right time

- The importance of follow-up

- Being a biblical witness with signs and wonders following

THE PROGRESSION OF THE RELIGIOUS SPIRIT

— Mark R. Anderson —

Published by Mark Anderson Ministries 2001

Jesus warned His close disciples of the negative fruit of the religious spirit. How much more do we need to heed the master's warning today and guard our hearts from an ungodly religious spirit? This book provides an in-depth study of Mark 7:1-13, including:

- How the religious spirit begins

- Finding fault: The first seed of the religious spirit

- Pride and false humility

- Holding onto man-made traditions

- Laying aside the commands of God

RELIGION OR RELATIONSHIP: WHICH ONE DO YOU WANT?
—— Mark R. Anderson ——

Published by Mark Anderson Ministries 2016

"I often wonder if religion is the enemy of God. It's almost like religion is what happens when the Spirit has left the building." – Bono U2 Band

Holy Spirit is moving powerfully all over the world. Yet the greatest opposition to the move of God is the religious spirit as it was when Jesus walked this earth. Jesus warned His disciples of the negative fruit of the religious spirit. How much more do we need to heed His warning today and guard our hearts from religion or the religious spirit? Mark writes about the importance of having the power of God in these last days but never permitting our gifts to overshadow our character. Mark shares about things that hindered his call and of powerful things that greatly impacted his life. Too many moves of God have been terminated prematurely because there was much emphasis only on gifting and the power given to man but little on character.

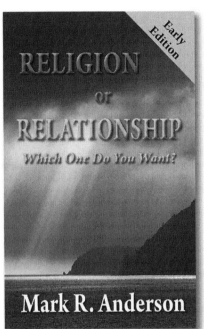

In this book Mark writes about how the religious spirit or religion can negatively impact all areas of society and on the contrary Christlike humility, integrity and relationship can have a positive effect. It can also usher in the glory of God, Heaven manifesting itself on Earth in signs, wonders and miracles like we have never seen or heard before. It's already here!

THE MOTIVATING FORCE OF PURPOSE

Mark R. Anderson

Published by Mark Anderson Ministries 2017

Are you motivated to go somewhere in life or ministry? Having concise purpose, vision and goals will help you conquer the mountains that stand in your way. See what effect purpose can bring in your life to motivate you in the right direction.

As you nail down vision and purpose in your life you will know your future, see it unfolding and know what direction to take in life. In this book we share practical insight from God's Word on how to fulfill a vision birthed from heaven. Having purpose and vision birthed by the Holy Spirit will help you easily navigate through the forks in the road and distractions that lay ahead. See and experience the motivating force of purpose in your life.

THE DAMAGING EFFECT OF THE RELIGIOUS SPIRIT IN POLITICS

—— Mark R. Anderson ——

Published by Mark Anderson Ministries 2016

If the foundations are destroyed, What can the righteous do (Psalms 11:3)? What will America look like on November 9, 2016, after the Presidential Election? America's Christian foundation has been eroding at a rapid pace. One major reason for this eroding is the disconnect between the average Christian and politics. How did this occur? Our founding leaders who birthed this great nation, the Constitution, freedom and liberty were very active politically and shed their blood for it's establishment.

Many of the founders were brave God loving and God fearing men. Sadly many Christians take what they gave us for granted by being apathetic when it comes to politics. Many Christians say God is in control and it will all work out, while sitting back and doing very little politically. As a result of this laid back attitude of Christians demonic strongholds have been set up in our nation's capitol with diabolical plans to remove God from this country. Will we turn this ship around before it is to late?

If Christians do not deal with issues like self righteousness, the religious spirit and the negative effect of Greek Philosophy in Western Christianity, in the area of politics we are plummeting towards extremely dark days in this country and around the world. As someone who ministers a great deal internationally I see most countries are greatly influenced by what happens in our nation's capitol. Christians who take on the right mindset when it comes to politics can greatly impact our nation and the world for the better.

In this book I share how we can restore this great land. We need to unite and get proactive instead of reactive when it comes to politics in America. Charles Finney ushered in the 2nd Great Awakening in the USA. He said "The time has come that Christians take consistent ground in politics. Christians have been exceedingly guilty in this matter. But the time has come when they must act differently. Christians seem to act as if they thought God did not see what they do in politics. But I tell you He does see it - and He will bless or curse this nation according to the course they [Christians] take [in politics]."

"Silence in the face of evil is itself evil: God will not hold us guiltless. Not to speak is to speak. Not to act is to act" - Pastor Dietrich Bonhoeffer. This book will reveal things regarding Christians and politics that very few are aware of. We can act, get knowledge and turn this country around before it is too late. It is time for the Paul Revere's to ride again.

MARK'S MUSIC

Check out Mark's music and download for free.

Mark Anderson

COME

Words and Music by
Mark R. Anderson

www.markandersonministries.
com/christian-music/check-out-
marks-latest-song-come

I love these moments in time with you my sweet Jesus.

I love these moments in time. Come Holy Spirit.

We come with open arms to embrace you Heavenly Father.

Chorus

Come Father, Son & Holy Spirit (2X).

Verse 2

Teach us all ways Father, Son and Holy Spirit.

Teach us to worship you in Spirit and in truth.

Come in all your glory Father, son and Holy Spirit.

Chorus

Come Father, Son and Holy Spirit (2X).

Made in the USA
Columbia, SC
29 April 2022

59663229R00098